Still Your Dad, Always My Son

A Year in the Life of a Grieving Father

David Contreras

ISBN 979-8-89428-699-0 (paperback)
ISBN 979-8-89428-700-3 (digital)

Christian Faith Publishing
832 Park Avenue
Meadville, PA 16335
www.christianfaithpublishing.com

Printed in the United States of America

Dedication

This book is dedicated to all my fellow grieving fathers. We live every day, week, month, and year with the unfortunate knowledge that our sons and/or daughters no longer reside with us here on earth. But that painful fact does not prevent us from reserving a special place in our hearts and our everyday thoughts as we move forward with our journey of grief.

The Lord is close to the brokenhearted, and
he saves those whose spirits have been crushed.
(Psalm 34:18 NCV)

Acknowledgments

I wish to thank my fellow member facilitators of GriefShare at Bayside Adventure Church. My wife and I have been blessed to share in this ministry with some of the most compassionate and devoted volunteers we have ever met. The commitment of these individuals who have heeded the call to walk alongside those in emotional pain caused by the death of their loved ones is a gift granted by God. Thank you. You do make a difference.

I also wish to thank my fellow grieving fathers who attend our monthly bereaved father's support group. Over the years, we have come together regularly, helping each other by sharing the mutual pain of our losses, and supporting each other in keeping our children alive in our hearts and in those of our families, friends, and the communities we live in. The compassion, empathy, and love that we share with each other only help to reinforce our ultimate goal to the world that our children shall never be forgotten.

I also want to thank Ron Harder, the original facilitator of our father's bereavement group. His support helped us dads to understand that in order to progress in our grief journey, it is important as men to recognize that it is okay to cry and to openly grieve. We do so that we may also be of support to our families and honor our children who now reside in heaven.

I especially want to give thanks to my wife, Kirsti; my son, JP; my daughter-in-law, Kimberly; and my grandson, Nicholai (Nick). You have all been so supportive of my efforts to share with other fathers who work through their grief day-to-day. Because of you, I have learned to allow myself to thank God for my yesterdays and my todays and to look forward to the hopes and dreams I still have for my tomorrows.

I would also like to acknowledge my late son, Nick. Though you may reside in heaven with our Lord, you still occupy a most prominent place in my heart, my everyday thoughts, and in how you influence the way I now see my world.

And most importantly, I want to acknowledge my wholehearted belief that God's planned reunion for Nick and I will forever keep him alive in my heart from where I reside now in my temporary home on earth. I thank you, Lord, for your loving and merciful hand in guiding me throughout my journey of grief and for giving me purpose to carry out the continued plans you have for me.

> So with you: Now is your time of grief, but
> I will see you again and you will rejoice, and no
> one will take away your joy. (John 16:22 NIV)

Introduction

A whole year can last a long time for us grieving fathers, especially when our grief occupies so much of our day-to-day lives. Because we are constantly aware of our loss, the many holidays, family celebrations, and social events can all become moments we would rather avoid now that our son or daughter will be missing from these festivities. I don't have to tell you that when you are grieving, getting through yesterday was hard, trying to get through today may not be much easier, and you likely have few if any plans for how to get through tomorrow as that day seems to be so far away. Beyond the days come the weeks that seem so very long and then the months, which seem to endlessly drag on and on, and any thought of what another year's worth of grief will look like only darkens any bright days we may be experiencing or hoping for in our minds.

The prospect of having to navigate through an entire year in our grief only adds more weight to our everyday heavy burdens, which include supporting our spouse who shares in our grief and raising our other children who may still be at home. Outside of home and family, we have our jobs and the demands of the workplace to deal with, as well as the other responsibilities we may feel obligated or expected to carry out, many of which we do not really want to do. And of course, there is our own personal grief that we must contend with as we attempt to channel through what others may think looks like any normal day, but what they may not understand is that for us grieving fathers, those normal days do not apply to our lives anymore.

This book is intended to remind grieving fathers that they are not alone in their grief, that what they are going through and feeling is normal, and that we don't have to be strong when we cannot. We are no less men because we allow others to walk alongside us, holding us up when we feel like falling, wiping away our tears when we cry, listening to us when we need to express our feelings, praying for us, loving us, and being our strength on those days when we know that we are too weak to even attempt to hide our pain.

Because grief is personal and unique to each one of us who has to go through it, no one can tell you how to get through it, and this book is not intended to do anything other than to be a source of encouragement. Through using some of my own experiences in my own grief journey as examples and recalling some of my observations of fellow grieving fathers who have and/or are going through their own grief process, I hope to share where I get my strength and how I choose to make it through my days, weeks, months, and years. And I hope that in my sharing with you a year of my life in grief as a dad, you, too, can find a safe and comforting path through which your journey will progress.

Because my son, Nick, died in January of 2011, the path of my annual grief journey always follows the traditional calendar year. My annual year of grief usually begins in January and concludes in December, and I have found that the end of one year of grieving usually sets up the beginning of a new one, creating a new chapter in what has become my annual journey of grief. This has been my ongoing annual emotional trek now for over twelve years.

In writing this book, I have purposely titled many of the chapters to include the months of the year. In each of those chapters, I have chosen to share not just what I may have experienced in any of those given months within this past year but also my experiences during any of the past twelve years since my son died. In the process, I am allowing you to see where I was, where I may be now, and where I may be headed during the different periods of my grief progress. And if by chance you find that any of my experiences may be similar to what you have already gone through or may be going through, I hope you will take it as a sign of God's assurance that you are not alone. I hope you will know that if you see that I was and am able to make it to the next step in my journey, then so will you in yours.

The pain of a grieving father is real and shared by many of us who have unfortunately traveled and continue to travel this same journey. Perhaps when days are feeling gloomy and hopeless for the grieving father, he can reach for this book and find some comfort through my own experiences and those of others, and they may be reminded that their child is in a good place. Knowing that the place they now reside is in heaven, allows us grieving fathers to feel joy for our child who is now in the presence of God. That knowledge allows fathers to mourn, yes, but it also allows us to celebrate and appreciate that our child's entire presence here on earth was a blessing and continues to be a blessing even from where they now reside in heaven.

When I began working through those early days, months, and even years of my grief journey, I yearned to find other fathers who knew this journey all too well. I needed to lean on them, ask questions, beg for answers, and receive guidance on how to get through the seemingly endless pain and sorrow. And despite the progress in our culture to tear down many of the traditional male-female attitudes toward those who grieve, I found that there was little out there to truly help those of us fathers who were going through the grief of losing their child as most sources I could find were often geared more toward women and mothers. With so few sources available, I hope that sharing my own experiences in this book can be of help to my fellow grieving fathers. Whether the grief is new or ongoing for many years, we all need to remind those around us that a father's love for his child, be they on earth or in heaven, is never-ending.

When my thirteen-year-old son, Nick, died, I initially failed in my attempts to fulfill the traditional male stereotype of the strong supportive man of the house by putting on the macho persona I thought was expected of me despite my own efforts to hold back my own tears and emotions. I felt it was my duty to be the rock of support to my family and to shield and protect my wife as the grieving mother. But instead, what I found was that she needed to grieve for our son Nick in her own way. What I needed to do was be supportive of how she grieved for him and understand that I could not fix what had happened, which is a normal male reaction. After all, how do you fix the death of your child?

The first step was to recognize that I, too, needed to grieve for Nick, and unless I could accept my personal loss of "my son," I was going to be of no use in being a supportive husband to my wife with regard to her personal loss for "her son." We both needed to respect our personal losses before we could successfully support each other in our combined loss for our son. Adding to the already immense suffering and mourning for our son and the grief that accompanied it, it was during my first year of grief that I also found myself in the position of attempting to give my wife, Kirsti, further support for what was to be the first of her three battles with cancer—an added burden on her that would add to but never replace her grief.

Kirsti's heroic fight to beat cancer aside, something else occurred as we embarked on what has become her journey of grief, my own journey, and our combined journey that I had not counted on that continues on through to the present. What I had not expected and what I do now accept is that the process of going through grief has no time line or limit, and most particularly, that grieving for your child will have no earthly finishing date. It will last for the rest of my life.

> Many are the plans in the mind of a man,
> but it is the purpose of the Lord that will stand.
> (Proverbs 19:21 ESV)

Chapter 1

The December Triggers
of a New Year

Many are the plans in a person's heart, but it
is the Lords purpose that prevails.
—Proverbs 19:21 NIV

This past December, just before Christmas, I took my grandson, Nicholai, to his evening swim practice because both his parents were working and unable to do so. The weather was very cold that evening, and everywhere you looked around the pool, it was wet due to a rainstorm that had passed through during the day. I was all layered up in sweatshirts and a heavy jacket as I sat shivering while sitting on the wet and uncomfortable aluminum grandstands that viewed the swimming pool lanes. Little did I know that I had set myself up for a trigger often associated with my grief.

As I sat on those cold aluminum bench seats, I found myself all alone as there were no other parents or grandparents who had joined me. Apparently, they had more common sense than this old displanted Southern Californian because instead of watching their kids/grandkids swimming on this very cold December evening, they chose to either read a book, sip on a hot drink, or take a snooze with their earbuds on while listening to music from their cell phones—all in the confines of their heated cars in the parking lot. I am not criticizing or judging them, but I am only wondering why I did not have the same common sense to do so as well.

Actually, I think I know why. Maybe it was the former coach in me who felt that it was only right to be out there if my grandson had to be. After all, compared to me, all he was wearing were his goggles and his swim jammers. Perhaps it was because when I grew up, I remember that was what my parents did for me. They, too, would watch me at my athletic practices or contests, often alone as well, showing me their support regardless of the conditions. Perhaps those experiences influenced me and my wife as we did the same for both of our sons who also swam competitively and played water polo. But in my grandson's case, it was more likely because I had promised to take him to McDonald's if he worked hard, and I thought I should be out there to see to it that he lived up to his end of the bargain.

As it so happened, he did work hard that evening, and I like to think it was because of my presence in the stands that he followed through with his promise. But to be honest, with all the steam coming off the heated water in the pool, he couldn't see me any better than I could see him. So I probably could have gotten away with joining the other parents or grandparents in the parking lot, sitting warmly in my own heated vehicle and either taking his word for it or pretending I saw his whole workout.

As I watched my grandson swim, I found myself reminiscing of similar cold December evenings in the past. I recalled watching his father, my older son, JP, and his uncle, my late younger son, Nick, doing the same. But what truly generated a stir of emotions in me was my observations at the end of the practice as the whole team took part in pulling the tarps across the water in order to cover up the pool lanes.

With the steam still rising from the heated water of the pool, I could make out bodies in the water pulling on the tarps, but I could not make out for sure which body was my grandson. But even though I could not see him, I knew he was out there because I could hear him. I heard a commanding, encouraging, and loud voice from the water barking out, "Let's go, everyone! One, two, three, pull! That's it! Let's do it again!" No, he wasn't in charge, and he wasn't the only one barking out commands. He was just being a member of the team, working together with his teammates and friends, as they all oddly seemed to be enjoying themselves.

My grandson was not being bossy; he was just playing his part by motivating his teammates to work together alongside him. At that moment, I closed my eyes, still hearing those words of encouragement in the pool. However, I no longer recognized the voice as that of my grandson. Instead, it was clearly my son Nick's voice echoing in my mind. It was as though he was touching his nephew from heaven, encouraging him to use the same words and efforts that he once did himself on those cold December nights eleven years before at the end of an intense swimming practice. And yes, I did take my grandson to McDonald's.

I share this story because the truth is that any thoughts of my son Nick can become an emotional trigger at any time and anywhere. Sometimes the trigger can feel painful, but as the years have passed by, I find that I have many more moments of happiness, joy, and good memories of the time he was here than in any dark place the pain that surrounds his death can pull me into. The triggers are no longer just sad reminders, but they are also the memories that help keep my son with me always, and they remind me that he is with me every day and every year. The process of grieving for my son is a lifelong journey with many climbs and descents, and its paths have many smooth and rough roads, but it is a journey I am fully committed to if for no other reason than I am still and forever Nick's dad.

> The sufferings we have now are nothing compared to the great glory that will be shown to us. Everything God made is waiting with excitement for God to show his children's glory completely. (Romans 8:18–19 NCV)

Chapter 2

•••—•———•———•—•••

January

Come to me, all of you who are tired and have heavy loads,
and I will give you rest. Accept my teachings and learn
from me, because I am gentle and humble in spirit, and
you will find rest for your lives. The burden that I ask you
to accept is easy; the load I give you to carry is light.

—Matthew 11:28–30

As January brings us into another new year, the feeling that we are having a hangover comes to mind as we begin what amounts to our emotional and physical recovery from having said goodbye to last year and the over-zealous manner in how we welcome in the new one. But nothing truly brings full acceptance that the holiday seasons are officially over than the dreaded symbolic post-holiday season cleanup and the taking down of the Christmas decorations. Unable to procrastinate any longer, we proceed with the unjoyful task of packing them away and returning them to storage and then turn our attention to the challenges that are our not-so-well-thought-out commitment to what we call New Year's resolutions.

New Year's resolutions are the annual practices of making promises and commitments to live better, get in shape, lose some weight, eat healthier, be more positive, worry less, make more friends, complete a new project, and well, you know, just have a better year than last year. Despite our best intentions, most of us rarely succeed in fulfilling the promises of our resolutions. But there is one thing that we can all agree on when it comes to the beginning of any new year, and that is the opportunities that it can bring. For some, January represents the opportunity to start afresh, leaving behind all that did not go well last year, like our real and perceived failures, sufferings, and our bad luck moments. But the promise of new opportunities allows us to look ahead, leaving behind what we want to forget while looking forward to all the possibilities of a better world and to the personal happiness that the "new" year may bring. But to those of us who are grieving fathers, January also means that another year will now commence, and it will do so without the physical presence of our beloved sons or daughters.

For a grieving father, it does not matter if this is their first year without their child or if this is another year beyond the first because, to a grieving father, any year without their child will never be as promising as they would hope, regardless of how long the distance in time when they passed away. But especially early on in their grief, a father will no doubt seemingly have those recurring ongoing thoughts that seem to repeatedly cross his mind, and the questions he will ask himself will always be centered on, "How am I going to make it through another year without my child?"

My name is David Contreras, and I am a grieving father who accepts that "grieving father" will always be one of my titles. My thirteen-year-old son, Nick, died in January of 2011, and that reminder is affecting my present mood as I begin to write this book while sitting at a local Peete's coffee shop in my hometown. Outside the sun is shining brightly through the window on this beautiful crisp morning, but I am not being as grateful as I should be for the God-given beauty he is providing for me today. At this moment, my personal preference for what a wintery January day should look like is that it should be gloomy, cloudy, dark, and cold. On this very morning, my attitude toward the month of January is being influenced by the fact that January will always be remembered as the month my son Nick passed away. Right now, all I can think of is that January is the month that we said goodbye to him in church, before God and those of us who loved him, during what was his celebration of life. To me,

January is the beginning of another year without him physically here on earth, and it is also the month that earmarks the moment that my lifetime journey of grief for him has begun.

Grief can be both emotionally and physically draining on a grieving father, and it is not rare for a father early on in their grief to eat too little or eat too much, to sleep too much or not sleep enough, and to work too little or to work too much. As for his emotional state, one can say that even during the best of times, the stress of everyday life can consume most of us. But when you add the trauma—that is grief—to what may already be the heavy burdens of emotional stress and physical strain on your mind and body, then the question you may end up asking yourself is, "How am I supposed to get through today, let alone tomorrow?"

I am a Christian man, and though it took me a while to realize it, I now believe that the answer to that question and the source of surviving each day in my journey of grief is and always has been right in front of me. All I had to do to find it was to open my eyes and my heart to the Lord. You see, I believe God knows when we are at our weakest, and because he knows our pain, he will welcome us into his arms and give us comfort when we need it most.

In the Bible, Matthew 11:28 lets us know that God invites us to lean on him when we can no longer do so on our own, especially when we feel we cannot face what the future may hold for us. As the new year begins to shape our emotional and mental state, we can feel that it is going to be a long year, and when you add to that the added burden of grief, it becomes evident that no grieving father has the emotional skills by which to navigate the year's journey ahead of them, no matter how strong we may feel we are or how strong others may think we are. It may be our year's journey, but thankfully, it is God who is leading the way, and it is he who will be our guide on the path before us.

> "Come to me, all of you who are tired
> and have heavy loads, and I will give you rest."
> (Matthew 11:28 NCV)

Chapter 3

God's Compassion for the Grieving Father

For no one is cast off by the Lord forever. Though he brings grief, he will show compassion, so great is his unfailing love. For he does not willingly bring affliction or grief to anyone.
—Lamentations 3:31–33 NIV

As fathers, we have this expectation of ourselves to be the protectors of our family, especially of our children. When they hurt, we heal them. When they are scared, we will protect them. But when we confront the death of our child, we may come to the point of losing confidence in ourselves. We look for the reason and rationality for what has happened, and at times, we may point our own finger back at ourselves, and in doing so, we often place blame upon the person we see in the mirror. We feel ashamed that we have failed as fathers to protect the most important gift God had entrusted to us—our child, who is now in heaven instead of in their bedroom, waiting for us to tuck them in and kiss them goodnight. Now we feel as though we must carry the burden of blame for everyone down the line, meaning our child, our wife, our family, and even God. We feel as though we have let them all down.

The prospect of living through a new year carrying this burden from which we feel guilt does not go unnoticed by God. He does not want us to live in constant pain, but he knows we will have pain. But he promises to never let us be alone in our grief. He will be there with us every step of the way.

> For he does not willingly bring affliction or
> grief to anyone. (Lamentations 3:33 NIV)

The emotional and physical pain we as parents may be going through during the onset of our grief seems unbearable. But history shows that parents do survive, do progress forward, and do understand that their child does live on in the glory of heaven and the embrace of the Lord.

> I consider that our present sufferings are
> not worth comparing with the glory that will be
> revealed in us. (Romans 8:18 NIV)

When our grief is fresh, we don't want to recognize that our present suffering will result in a glorious conclusion as Romans 8:18 suggests. We don't want to accept that the loss of our child is needed to reveal God's glory to us or to the world. I can recall one day pulling over in my car after work on my way home, tears in my eyes, screaming at God, "Why did you take him? He wasn't hurting anyone! He was a good kid! Why him? Why not someone else's kid!" Does that sound selfish? Of course, it is, but I meant every word of it when I thought and screamed it in my car at that particular moment. But in my defense, I was a father in very deep pain who only wanted his son back. I was in no mood to try and understand the comparing of how the world would be a better place and the lives of my son and I—then, now, and when we are gone—were to reveal God's glory. My only thoughts were, "How can I go on like this? If God had intended for me to be Nick's dad, then why would he take him from me when our relationship as father and son wasn't done? If my purpose in life was to be the father of two sons, then why will there only be one son to bury me when I die?"

> The King was shaken. He went up to the
> room over the gateway and wept. As he went, he
> said, "O Absalom! My son, my son Absalom! If
> only I had died instead of you—O Absalom my
> son, my son!" (2 Samuel 18:33 NIV)

Early in my grief, while in prayer, I remember asking God, "Lord, why didn't you take me instead of Nick?" I remember sharing with my wife that I had prayed that question, and her response to me made one of the greatest impacts on me as a Christian man, husband, and father that she could have ever given me. She told me, "Because God doesn't think you are ready. God took Nick because he was ready." That was hard for me to hear, and I am sure it was hard for her to say, but reluctantly, I knew then as I do now that it was true.

As the years have rolled on for me during my journey of grief, I have come to accept and be comforted by the presence of God in my life and how he has led me through scripture to make sense of and understand that he is in control. I can now accept more so that he has always been in control and that my life without my son still has meaning, and that includes Nick as well.

> "I say this because I know what I am plan-
> ning for you," says the Lord. "I have good plans
> for you, not plans to hurt you. I will give you
> hope and a good future. (Jeremiah 29:11 NCV)

In most of my life's personal struggles and not just those of grieving for my son, I have come to lean on Jeremiah 29:11. When work promotions passed me by or when my best laid-out plans failed or when worries over my wife's three battles with cancer seemed unsurmountable and when I watched unable to help my older son from the sidelines as he experienced the downsides of the grown-up world, I usually found that the endgame of those struggles had a purpose and that God provided me the answers with a positive outcome. Eventually, I could see that God's plan always had priority over those of my own, and I could see that he was revealing that truth to me in

Jeremiah 29:11—but not at first, not immediately after my son Nick died.

It took me quite a while to see how in any way Jeremiah 29:11 could possibly apply to losing my son, especially at first glance. "I will give you hope and a good future." How in the world could life without my son give me hope when he was not with me any longer? And a good future? What did I have to look forward to? I know many would have said to me, and I agree that there was my wife and older son to think about, but even in the midst of being grateful for the presence of my wife, she still almost died from cancer three times all while in the midst of grieving for our son. As for my older son, JP, yes, he is my world, but I always assumed that I was supposed to be sharing that world with both him and his brother, Nick.

> Very truly I tell you, you will weep and
> mourn while the world rejoices. You will grieve,
> but your grief will turn to joy. (John 16:20 NIV)

There came a point early in my grief when I came face-to-face with a term that became my reality, and it took me a while to truly understand it for myself, let alone try to explain it to others who were around me. If you go through any kind of grief counseling or take part in any kind of supportive grief program, one of the key phrases often introduced to describe what you are now embarking on in your journey is the term "new normal." From the moment I first heard it, its definition has continuously evolved and has caused so many varying reactions from those around me, constantly reminding me of the different path I had originally thought I was on and constantly updating itself as I reach every new fork in the road of my life.

How did this "new normal" apply to me? First, there was the reality that my life had forever been changed. A very important piece of my life was now missing as though a limb from my body was no longer attached. I would never look the same, nor would I ever be the same. My approach to life was now altered, and it was visibly notice-able to some who knew me well and hardly noticed by others who did not, but it was definitely ingrained in my physical and emotional psyche. It may have taken a while for me to understand it, but the impact of it was immediate. It meant there is a new me and it is my new normal.

Secondly, my everyday routines and my everyday thinking process have all changed, and for the most part, they are not likely to return to where they were prior to my son going on to heaven. No longer would we greet each other when I got home from work, and my regular routine of physically saying good night to him at bedtime or goodbye every morning before I went to work has now stopped. I used to always go into his room and tell him he was the best thirteen-year-old boy in the whole wide world and that his daddy loved him. And though I would eventually resume that morning practice before I left for work until the day I retired, I did so now symbolically, speaking to an empty bed and kissing a vacant pillow goodbye. My daily prayers of asking God to watch over both my boys and keep them safe from harm every day now changed forever. I still say that same prayer for my older son, JP, even as he is now married and a father himself, but for Nick, it has changed to my asking God to watch over my son with him in heaven. I ask God to please remind Nick not to worry because in God's years, I will see him tomorrow. And every day, I ask God to relay that I miss him and that I love him.

Thirdly is the acceptance that there is nothing I can do, nor is there anything anyone else can do to change what has altered my life forever as I have now evolved into what is my "new normal." And though I know that happiness will still come and go, the reality is that my son Nick is no longer here for me to hug, kiss, talk to, and see him grow into a man. However, that doesn't mean he has no presence in my life, for he is always present and constantly in my heart and is always in my everyday thoughts. I won't say that things are now all better, but they are no longer getting worse; and I do have many more good days than bad ones, and I now know that God's planned path for me has never changed.

The path God has set for me is still on the same route as before, but like all journeys, if you stay on the same road for a long time, the scenery will change. And now that my son is in heaven, the view on my path has changed. The new scenery that everyone sees me traveling on is now my new normal, and everything that is familiar in my life now seems to look so different.

> If anyone belongs to Christ, there is a new creation. The old things have gone; everything is made new. (2 Corinthians 5:17 NCV)

Every January, I can sense new progress in my grief journey. At first, the month of January only brought me sad memories of losing my son, but as time has passed, the date of his death has evolved into what we call his *angelversary*. I have come to love that word, angelversary, because it marks the day he was blessed to go home to be in the glorious presence of the Lord. His angelversary has helped me to no longer just see the month of January in the negative, and it has opened my heart to cherish more the happiness of recalling when I had him here and not let the horrible day he left us overwhelm me. But even with all of the progress I have accomplished during my grief, I am still a humbled earthly man and father, and within any given year, I will have those moments when I am confronted with the heartbreaking absence of my son, who no longer resides with us here in this world.

Every year, around January 13, on Nick's angelversary, my sister and brother-in-law, Linda and Mark, spend a weekend in San Francisco with us. Together we enjoy a place where Nick loved to go with his mom, brother, and me; and we do things he enjoyed doing when we visited as a family, and we reminisce about Nick. Together we celebrate Nick's having been here for thirteen years and all that he meant to us then and what he means to us now. As I am writing this after our most recent trip to San Francisco, it has come to my attention and is now very much on my mind that next year will be his thirteenth angelversary. He will have been gone from this earth as long as he was in it, and I do not know how my wife and I will react come next January. But God has always been there for us to ease our anxieties when it comes to grieving for Nick by insuring us of his love and by giving us the knowledge that our son is safely and lovingly in his arms.

I am a fan of sorts of the Christian author and pastor, Max Lucado. I used to read his children's stories to both my boys when they were little, and I have since read a few of his other books that are aimed at us adults. One of his books that I have had for years is a daily devotional titled *Grace for the Moment* that I still read occasionally when I am looking for daily inspiration. It so happens that on the day of January 13, 2023, while we were on our recent angelversary weekend marking twelve years to the day Nick went to heaven, I opened Lucado's devotional to the page marked "January 13." The page was titled, "Thinking of You." The scripture of the day was from Philippians 4:6: "Pray and ask God for everything you need, always giving thanks." And Lucado's opening sentence was, "Heaven knows no difference between Sunday mornings and Wednesday afternoon." He also added in his own words, "You may go days without thinking of him, but there's never a moment when he is not thinking of you."

The devotional is about thinking of God in heaven, knowing that he thinks of you every day. But God works in so many ways, and I believe through Lucado, God used that day's devotional and the scriptures attached to it to remind me that he is my heavenly father and that here on earth I am always JP and Nick's father too. As he quoted from scripture, "Be constant in prayer" (Romans 12:12 NIV), and "Let heaven fill your thoughts" (Colossians 4:2 TLB), I remembered that I do pray every day, asking God to protect my older son, JP, and his family. I remembered that I do fill my thoughts with heaven every day because that is where God sits and looks after me and my loved ones and that is where he has my son Nick in his loving arms. As always, I entered into my private journal and my Facebook private group page, "Nick, today marks twelve years to the day I last saw you here on earth. I know where you are, son. I know where you are. You are the best thirteen-year-old boy in the whole wide world. Your daddy loves you."

As another new year begins and my grief journey continues and knowing that it will be another eleven months before I return to the point of reassessing my year's progress, I will continue to look to God to get me through the year. As fathers, our grief will not cease upon reaching the end of a day, a week, or even a month. And I know that

God will provide me the strength to continue moving forward, that it will be him who will hold me up when I cannot stand, and that it will be in his arms that I can cry in as another year of missing my son Nick will have begun.

> For no one is cast off by the Lord forever. Though he brings grief, he will show compassion, so great is his unfailing love. For he does not willingly bring affliction or grief to anyone. (Lamentations 3:31–33 NIV)

Chapter 4

February

I have no one in heaven but you. I want nothing on
earth besides you. My body and my mind are weak,
but God is my strength. He is mine forever.
—Psalm 73:25–26 NCV

On February 14, 2011, just thirty-one days after my son Nick passed away, my wife, Kirsti, my older son, JP, and me found ourselves sitting in an Italian restaurant that we had frequented for years for a Valentine's Day meal. I don't know why we did it. I cannot even remember if it was my idea, my wife's, or both. All I know is that we did not feel comfortable being there, and we didn't enjoy it. My son JP, in the beginning of his own grief journey, did not want to be there either, and the way he was dealing with it was by being difficult and angry. I would have lost it on him if it hadn't been for the fact that I wasn't feeling that much different because, like him, I didn't want to be there either. Once we were there, we just knew it was a mistake. We tried to eat, but we had very little appetite. So we paid our bill and collected our leftovers, and we went home.

I guess for some reason we felt like we had to go through the motions of this annual holiday. It was an utterly failed attempt at beginning our new normal. It was very evident to us that there were only three of us at the restaurant table that evening. When we got home, we had to confront the realization once again that the fourth member of our family, our son and brother Nick, was still not there. Despite our efforts, we were not yet ready to fully accept the proverbial empty chair at our dining table that represented Nick, the missing member of our family.

Being so close to when Nick died and when we had his celebration of life, like any other father in my place, I found myself pleading to God continuously, "I need help, Lord! Please tell me how this new normal is supposed to work." I had never experienced anything like this before. I recalled the sorrow of losing my mother and two of my grandparents, but my grief process in those instances was nowhere close to what I was experiencing after losing my son. I could accept their passing as a natural part of life that is to be expected. But losing your child? A part of you dies when you lose your child, and that part of you never really comes back to life. And whatever your new normal will look like, you are forever going to be a grieving father.

About a year or two into my grief, I met a fellow grieving father who shared how he and his wife, after losing their youngest child, planned for and had another child. He told me that their train of thought was that they are supposed to have four kids, and so they had another child. He said that their new child brought them joy, but it didn't take away any of the pain of losing their deceased child. In their thoughts at that time, their new child was to "symbolically" take the place vacated by their missing fourth child and ease their pain, but before you judge them, that's not what happened.

What he later came to believe was that God gave to him and his wife their "fifth" child, not to replace the one in heaven but rather to be an addition to their family on earth. Their new child became an added blessing, not a replacement for their one child in heaven who would never leave their hearts. That is when he truly knew that the grieving would go on and that their new normal would always reflect that they now had five children, but the fourth one was in heaven.

As for me, that first month after my son died, I was still in the waning days of shock, and I had no idea how I was supposed to function in my new normal. It would take that whole first year of my grief to progress slowly and accept God's presence during the darkest moments of my pain and sorrow. In that year, I came to recognize that God was providing me encouragement and support through individuals and/or groups he was placing before me to walk alongside of me as I moved forward in my grief journey.

My son Nick has been in heaven for twelve years now, and at the end of each year of his passing, I am able to look back on how my grief has progressed. This is easy enough for me to do as I have kept a private journal ever since the early days of my grief, writing to my son as if he were with me still, and I have also facilitated a private Facebook group blog that I post in regularly. At times, I have looked back at some of my journal entries and/or past postings in my Facebook private group, and I can see that I have made a lot of positive forward movement every year. However, I don't just look back on how I have progressed from year to year, but I also take time to look forward and see where my journey may lead me to during the coming years. Whether I look back or forward though, what really intrigues me is how I consider what part my son Nick will continue to play in my life from this time forward.

As a father, in raising my kids, I always used to look back during the new year and reflect on the growth of my boys. I looked back with pride on how much they grew physically, emotionally, intellectually, maturitywise, and I looked to the future both with anticipation and with plenty of parental concern to envision what was in store for them in the coming year. I always prayed for their good health and their safety and that I as their father would be supportive in their endeavors and protect them from any harm. That last one always gets to me though. "Protecting them from harm" is always so hard to come to grips with when I experience those pangs of guilt that can hit you during your grief.

No matter the time of year a father may lose their child, I believe that the second month plays a major transitional role in the early stages of grief as it did for me. During that second month, the initial shock from when my son died was still lingering, and the months soon to follow, I could tell, were going to take up much of my emotional and physical energy just as I was entering a new phase of my bereavement. In my case, be it looking back or to the present, February seems to be a perfect second month for my grief years because they traditionally still have those cloudy, cold, and wintery weather days. A sunny day that might appear may make my physical body appreciate the warmth, but in my mind and in my heart, I still have days when both may still ache, and I will feel no reason to celebrate a beautiful day because the gloomy weather still feels appropriate.

Around the time my wife and I entered our second month of grief, we sought and began attending support groups such as Compassionate Friends, Bereaved Parents of the USA, and GriefShare through our church. At the time, it was still close to the time of our son's death, and we were still fortunate to have family and friends who had yet to move on with their own lives and who were still present if not physically, then at least emotionally via all forms of communication, continuing to give us much-needed support. But it was becoming very evident that what we really needed was to be with others who knew the kind of pain we were experiencing. We also began counseling as a family and as a married couple and eventually as individuals. But we quickly realized that it was our individual grief that also needed attention and that would have to be addressed by each of us on our own.

It didn't take me long to realize that what I needed was to be with other grieving dads. Very early on in my grief, I was blessed and fortunate to have support from other men close to me—be it from my family such as my dad; my brother; brothers-in-law; or even from any of the men who were close friends of mine who loved me, prayed for me, and gave me emotional support. But as much as I was appreciative and blessed to have that support, there was only so much they could provide me as a man because they fortunately never had to go through this experience themselves (and I would never want them to).

I have known of men who had lost a child, but other than a couple of specific individuals, I had never really witnessed a grieving father going through the grief process. So I sought a support group that could be more specific to me, the grieving dad, because I was lost and I needed to know that I wasn't alone and that I wasn't going insane. I googled and found some grief support groups, but most were geared toward a general grieving population as a whole, such as GriefShare, whom we eventually found to be a safe place of support to get through our grieving process. But as for grieving parents of children, most support groups to be found were for grieving mothers, and few, if any could be, found for the grieving father.

Just as I was about to jump into the darkness of despair over the possibility that I may have to do this alone, I was saved when a fellow grieving father approached me about joining his father's bereavement group. He happened to be the owner of the funeral home that provided us with services for my late son. The father's bereavement group he started was associated with the Bereaved Parents of the USA. I have been forever thankful for its existence since. From this group I have learned that I am not alone, I am not going insane, and that there are others who have walked my path and are still walking my path. And we are reinforced not just as grieving men but more importantly with the knowledge we will always be our children's father even if they are in heaven.

I have met with this group consistently every month for over twelve years, and I have even taken over as its facilitator from my friend who started it when he had to step back due to health issues. I can say that even now, after all this time, I feel blessed to be able to be of support for other grieving fathers, and by doing so, I continue to find support from them in my own continued journey as well.

> Brothers and sisters, we want you to know about those Christians who have died so you will not be sad, as others who have no hope. (1 Thessalonians 4:13 NCV)

Chapter 5

And Presidents Grieve Too

There will come a day, I promise you, when the thought of your
son, or daughter, or your wife or your husband, brings a smile
to your lips before it brings a tear to your eye. It will happen.
My prayer for you is that day will come sooner than later.

—Joe Biden

February is the month we celebrate President's Day, and among the men who have served as our presidents, there have been twenty-five of them who have experienced losing a child, and some have lost more than one. I believe what we can learn from that knowledge is that these men, despite their political power and their destined place in history, are not shielded from the emotional struggles of being a grieving father of a child in heaven. And that goes for all of us regardless of what our station in life is. Like any of us, even a president may wish to keep the memory of their child alive and share how their child is still among us.

I came upon this beautiful letter posted on the *Today Show* website from the late former president George H. W. Bush. It was written to his wife, Barbara, after they had lost their only daughter, Robin, to cancer shortly before her fourth birthday in 1958.

There is about our house a need. We need
some soft blonde hair to offset those crew cuts.

We need a doll house to stand firm against our forts and racquets and thousand baseball cards. We need someone who's afraid of frogs. We need a little one who can kiss without leaving egg or jam or gum. We need a girl.

We had one once—she'd fight and cry and play and make her way, just like the rest. But there was about her a certain softness. She was patient. Her hugs were just a little less wiggly.

But she is still with us. We need her and yet we have her. We can't touch her and yet can feel her. We hope she'll stay in our house for a long, long time.

Love, Pop.

When I read this letter, what I see is a heartfelt tribute from a grieving father for the daughter who has left them, but at the same time, he reminds his wife that their little girl is actually still with them and that she will never leave them.

President George H. W. Bush died seven months after his wife, Barbara, had passed away in 2018. And as a grieving father who shares the loss of a child with my wife, I can't tell you how much it touches my heart to know that George and Barbara Bush both chose to be buried next to their daughter, Robin. I can't help but feel that while many others grieved and mourned their loss to their family and friends of this world, they in turn were rejoicing for the reunion they had been anticipating and looking forward to for sixty years. I am overjoyed for both of them in that they are now together with their little girl once again in heaven. I can truly see God's hand in the joyous conclusion of their journey in grief.

In some of my past postings on Facebook and in my book *Forever 13*, I have shared about how President Joe Biden still grieves for the loss of his baby daughter Naomi—who died with his first wife, Nelia, in an automobile accident—and years later by the death of his adult son Beau, who died of brain cancer. I have also shared about President

Abraham Lincoln's loss of his young son Eddie before he was elected president and that of his young son Willie, who died while Lincoln was serving as president during the Civil War. In doing so, I am convinced that God does not distinguish between political beliefs when it comes to the grief for a child. God loves the grieving parents equally, and he openly makes room for their children in heaven.

> Jesus said, "Let the little children come to me, and do not hinder them, for the kingdom of heaven belongs to such as these." (Matthew 19:14 NIV)

I can relate to any father who makes a daily attempt to keep his child alive in his mind, in his heart, or in any way he so chooses. Not a day goes by that my wife and I will not mention our son Nick's name in some conversation and/or in sharing thoughts of him and, by doing so, making a conscious effort to keep him alive in our daily family routines. I myself have repeated daily as a closing statement whenever I write in my Facebook group account or in my personal journal the following phrase:

> "Nick, you are the best thirteen-year-old boy in the whole wide world. Your daddy loves you."

That grieving fathers can openly share and be empathetic for others who share such a tragic loss, it gives me hope that I can make it through yet another year of missing my son, and if you too are a grieving father, you too can openly and honestly let the world know that you miss your sons or daughters as well. I believe that showing true and sincere empathy to a fellow grieving father is a gift from God, even if they happen to have once been or are the president of the United States.

> He comforts us in all our troubles so that we can comfort others. When they are troubled, we will be able to give them the same comfort God has given us. (2 Corinthians 1:5 NLT)

Chapter 6

March

Humble yourselves, therefore, under God's mighty
hand, that he may lift you up in due time. Cast all
your anxiety on him because he cares for you.
—1 Peter 5:6–7 NIV

I remember returning to work a little less than five weeks after my son passed away. It was technically during the end of the second month, February, but it would be in the third month, March, that I would feel the weight of my anxiety in my attempts to return to work in my new normal state. In the United States, there are too many places of employment in my opinion that are not very sympathetic, be it on purpose or not, to the grieving worker. I was fortunate to not be in that position. I was a high school teacher, and my boss at the time had himself gone through grieving alongside his wife for his stepson, and he had empathy for me in my loss. He allowed me time off using accrued comp time, and he let me know that I could return when I felt ready. For that, I was forever grateful.

In hindsight, I realized that I was not ready to return to work when I did. As a grieving dad, I felt the need to continue trying to figure out how I was supposed to move forward and face the world without my son Nick in it. As I look back on it now, I realized that the working conditions and responsibilities I had as a teacher and the athletic director at my school, did me no favors, and only complicated all my efforts in balancing what I believed to be my effectiveness at work and my grief recovery at the same time.

But along with being a grieving dad for a son in heaven, I still had to be an earthly dad for my high schooler who was still at home. I still had the responsibility along with my wife, to continue raising our older son JP. I still felt the fatherly duty and even need to protect him, to be supportive of him, and to make parenting decisions based on what was over-all best for him in preparing for adulthood.

Shortly after Nick's celebration of life, we sent JP back to school and expected him to continue his studies as well as compete for his swim team, all while still working through his own grief for his brother. I can remember during those weeks taking long walks and passing by his school, leaving notes in his car in the school parking lot, still feeling that gut wrenching in my stomach, and always worrying about him. And yes, the loss of Nick created in me an almost panicky need to overcompensate in my worries for my older son, JP. What I failed to see as his father was that what he needed was to see some sense of normality from his parents, even if it was in their new normal. So I went back to work even though I felt it wasn't the right time yet, but I did it for JP.

As a grieving father, I paid the price for coming back to work too soon after my younger son's passing away, but the price of my older son's piece of mind was always a higher priority than my own piece of mind in my opinion. I returned to my old routine of very early morning hours in my athletic director's office, then I would write my lesson plans for the classes I taught. And after teaching my classes, I would then return to my office and work more on athletic business. I did much of this while avoiding all but my closest friends and the students in my classroom and any coaches who came by needing my assistance. I have never asked, but all my colleagues had to notice the change in me and how I was nowhere near my old self. And the punch in my gut feeling only got worse as my day moved along, and by lunchtime, with the blessing of my boss, I was usually in my car and on the road back home.

Throughout that first March, my drive home was often a blur, and frankly, I stopped quite a few times on the way home to sit and cry on the side of the road because I needed to just catch my breath, because I was hyperventilating. It was during one of those stops that I had my tirade with God that I mentioned before, and then there was another time that I pulled over and just sat in my car in silence for almost half an hour before realizing I had never turned off my car. Lucky for me I had put it in park.

During a two-week period not too long after I returned to work, I got two speeding tickets, and I got into an accident when I rear-ended a car at a signal light, not realizing that the car ahead of me had not yet taken off when the light turned green. To this day, I am thankful to God that no one was hurt. Ironically, I was only two miles from my house on what would have been the end of a round trip two-hundred-mile drive to and from an athletic director's meeting I had been attending when it occurred.

For an entire year, my drives home consisted of me bypassing the main highway, driving on back country roads, and at all costs, avoiding driving by my son Nick's school. I recall more than once pulling into the driveway when I got home and just sitting in my car for quite some time, trying to remember, "What did I do today?" or even more worrisome, "How did I get home?" And there were times I just didn't want to go inside the house yet, knowing Nick wasn't going to be there to welcome me home.

When attending my older son's, JP's, high school swim meets, I tried to avoid eye contact with just about everyone, not being sure how I would react or even worse, if others showed no reaction and I might feel really hurt or angry. When my wife and I attended church, we purposely walked in late and walked out early. I sometimes wished I stuck around because I needed sympathy from others, but I knew I wasn't ready to be around big crowds, and I definitely wasn't yet in the mood for small talk and socializing, even in church. And it hurt me to see my wife crying, be it at church or at any time. Being much aware of her telling me I couldn't make the crying stop, I still felt that bit of guilt that as the man of the family, as her spouse, and as JP's dad, I couldn't fix this. But as I was learning, you can't fix broken hearts. All you can do is try and make them stronger with the wounds still in them and move forward.

This was my first March after Nick died. I was constantly nervous thinking about what was happening to me, but I knew God was there for me. And like in all things, he watched after me, he protected me from harm, and he relieved me of many moments of anxiety.

I did get to witness that some goodness still existed in this world despite my emotional pain. And I know that God had a hand in reminding me that he was in control and he would not let me fall as he helped to restore in me the knowledge that his presence could also be found in others and their actions toward me.

There was the day my boss asked me to stay for a staff meeting one day after school so that my fellow staff members could present me with a guitar that my son Nick had started in his school's woodshop and that his teacher had finished for him. It presently hangs next to another guitar Nick made in the woodshop on our living room wall. At their end-of-season banquet, the girls basketball team all signed a poster board with well-wishes and condolences and presented it to me.

One day at school, I was informed that the school yearbook would be dedicated to me in memory of my son Nick, and there was also a ceremony put on by his woodshop teacher at his school that he was remembered and honored at. And while attending meetings of the State Executive Committee and Federated Council of the California Interscholastic Federation (CIF)—these are the body's that govern high school sports in the state of California—they recognized my loss and had a moment for my son.

Though I have had better months of March over the years since, that first one after my son's death I think truly reflected my state of mind at the time and my ill-fated readiness to literally take my new normal out for a drive too soon. But when you are a grieving father and you have responsibilities to not just keep your child in heaven alive in your heart but also to the well-being of your children still on earth and to continue with your responsibilities at home and the workplace, it can become overwhelming to get through it, but I survived it. But to do so, I had to let God take care of me. Because you cannot do it by yourself. Sorry, my brothers, but that is the truth. You cannot do it by yourself.

Just like some of my drives home were a blur, so was much of that first March. But as many of us get through that third month during any of our years in grief, we finally have to realize as well that it may seem for a while that we are now alone; we never really are.

> I leave you peace; my peace I give you. I
> do not give it to you as the world does. So don't
> let your hearts be troubled or afraid. (John 14:27
> NCV)

Chapter 7

April

Even though I walk through the valley of the shadow
of death, I will fear no evil, for you are with me;
your rod and your staff, they comfort me.

—Psalm 23:4 ESV

It took a while, but I have come to truly believe that my son's thirteen years here on earth were a full life. Where others may believe he was taken too soon or that he died before his time, I say that in no way was my son Nick cheated out of a full life. At one time perhaps, my wife and I, as well as others who love him, may have felt that we were cheated for not having him here longer, but reluctantly, I know there is no way that God has cheated him out of more time here on earth.

God has made it known to me that Nick's life had meaning and that he left this world leaving us with so much love. Nick fulfilled what God had planned for him, and then God took him home. And that is where I will see him again when God so chooses to reunite us. But till then, the grieving will continue.

By my first April after Nick's death, the blanketing fog that God provided us as a shield from emotional shock and a total mental breakdown began to lose much of its density. This also coincided with the period of time in which many of the family and friends who were providing us with emotional support, through no fault of their own, began to move on with their lives. By their moving on, they unknowingly left us on our own to begin much of the grief work that needed to be done.

Neither my wife nor I were upset, angry, or even hurt by the fact that many of those who had been there for us had moved on with their lives. But as that support dwindled, I was not prepared for the possibility of a lengthy and painful struggle that lay before me and my wife as we embarked on our first solo steps in our journey of grief for our son Nick. Had it not been for the early grief support we had sought out such as the private counseling, our GriefShare support group at church, and my monthly father's bereavement group, I believe the long and painful struggle I mentioned before would have overwhelmed me. I believe that without these sources of grief support, my alternative would have been for me to go at it alone, working through the many processes of grief by myself.

Thanks to hindsight, I can truly say that there is no grieving father who has the strength to accomplish such a task or so difficult a journey on their own. What I did come to realize was that I am capable of asking God for his help and letting him lead me to where I need to be and, when necessary, to whom I need to be with. And by the time my first April without Nick had come and gone, I found myself in the company of good men with whom I shared the unfortunate distinction of being grieving fathers.

My participation in a monthly father's bereavement group has not been the only avenue of support that I have sought out and used to work through my grief, but it has been one of the most valuable and consistent means of support that I could have ever been associated with and taken part in. Once a month for the past eleven years, this group has blessed me with their support, and I in turn hope that I have been able to return the favor.

As I mentioned earlier in this book, early on in my grief, I recognized I needed to be with other grieving fathers. I yearned to hear how other dads survived the loss of their child. How did they make it through today only to wake up the next morning and have to get through another day? How did they keep from falling apart when they heard their child's name, saw their picture on the wall, or ran into one of their child's friends? How or what did they do to ensure that their child would never be forgotten? How did they deal with the guilt of a father who could not prevent what had happened and who could not fix it for all concerned? As helpful as the facilitators at GriefShare were or empathetic family and friends were, sometimes you just need to be with other grieving parents who truly know. And more specifically, I needed to be with other grieving dads who knew.

I spoke earlier of the gentleman who started the father's bereavement group that I am associated with. He was the co-owner of the funeral home that handled all the arrangements for my son's celebration of life service. He was a former pastor who felt called by God to start a funeral home after he lost his adult son. When I visited him and his funeral home only a couple of days after my son Nick died, I was truly blessed. His empathy was genuine, and his sympathy felt truly personal. I could see he cared for me and my wife and wanted to be of support in any way he could because he understood the emotions and pain that we were going through, because he had experienced those same emotions himself. He would be the one who called me later to invite me to be part of the father's bereavement group.

Sometimes, being among men in a social gathering can be an interesting and at times entertaining experience to behold. First comes the sizing up of each other, followed by the sharing of and/or at times the embellishing of who we are, what skills we have, who we know, and what knowledge we supposedly possess. And we do this all in the name of staking our claim in the world of manhood, which most often can result in a room full of rolling eyes. None of us men are immune to revealing our competitiveness when expressing the "expertise" we claim to have on issues such as sports, politics, and the "I caught a fish this big" stories. And who hasn't stretched the tales of their own life's accomplishments, which seem to grow more and more in stature and folklore as we get older, or have a few too many beers in us?

But be it good-natured or all in fun, all that machismo seems to be less important when we are a father who has had to experience burying any of our sons or daughters. The willingness to share that experience with others can be more frightening than being called out on any tall-tale story we may have embellished. Because unlike any stretching of the truth in a male "just for fun of it" self-bragging competition, the love we have for our deceased child and the pain of that loss we now carry with us is genuine. And any strength in dealing with that pain in a public format of any type just wasn't built into the stereotype upbringing many of us men were instilled with in our secular world.

The first time our father's bereavement group met, I was of the illusion that I would either speak too much or not at all. As men, we never want to seem to look weak, and we definitely did not want to be seen crying in public or even worse, doing so in front of other men. And the potential for any of this to happen when meeting with others who also fear showing these same emotions are generally pretty good.

The general rule when meeting in any grief sharing group is that you are under no obligation to speak unless you wish to or until you feel ready to do so, and this same rule applied to the father's bereavement group as well. We were fortunate that our facilitator as a funeral home owner and grieving father himself had experienced what we were going through and likely anticipated how as men we might have fears in participating in such a group. But he eased our worries, showed great empathy, and set the tone early—a process we have used for the past eleven years.

I am at present the facilitator of this group due to the founder of the group having to back out for health reasons, but we have continued the same introductory methods he used to ease the anxiety or fears of any new father who attends our meetings. We introduce who we are, our child's name, when they passed away, and if we choose to do so, we can give the cause of death. By following this method, we are letting the new members know they are not alone. We have gone through what they are going through. We also establish that it does not matter among us how old their child was, and unless he wishes to discuss the cause of death, all that matters to all of us is that we are all grieving fathers. And though we may not grieve the same as each other, we know what it feels like to bury our child. A saying we often share is that, "We are all members of an exclusive club that none of us wished to be a member of, but we are glad to be here for each other."

What we have found is even if for just one day a month, our group is a safe place to gather together and be of support, get support, and have that shoulder to cry on—be it in real-time tears or symbolically. We know at these times we are not alone. The pain, the thoughts, the concerns, and the emotions we are going through are not just ours alone, and we often leave the meeting better for having been there than not at all. It doesn't take long for any of us to know that we don't have to wear the male armor of machismo and we can be just as strong leaning on others who understand the same pain, sorrow, and emotional state as the rest of us. There may be times we meet with a large group and other times when there are only a few, and then there are the times when we find that the best meetings occur when there are only two of us present. At those times, it is as though God knows the attention needed to be focused on one of us only. In all the years we have met, I have never had a meeting I wasn't grateful to have attended.

As I stated previously, this is not intended to be a "how to book," and I am not encouraging you to find such a group as mine; but rather, my only wish is to share how it has helped both me during my journey as well as those of other grieving fathers whom I have met these past years within this group. Should you search for and find such a group however, I will admit to praising God for answering my prayers that other grieving dads will know they too can get comfort and support from other dads who truly know what we are going through.

Wherever you are in your grief, especially when it is fresh, you can be assured it won't always feel so dark and gloomy. I can still recall at the end of the first father's bereavement meeting I attended that as we were about to close in prayer, our facilitator—no doubt sensing that our emotions were still uneasy—provided us with these encouraging words:

> It won't always feel this way. It won't always
> hurt this bad. You will laugh and smile again, and

in time the pain and tears won't come so often.
They may never completely go away because you
will always love and miss your child. But it will
get better. You will get better.

I have heard that message echoed if not word for word, then
in some shape or form with other bereavement groups often. Those
words not only helped me as I have moved forward in my grief, but I
have also shared them with other grieving parents who felt lost in the
beginning of their grief journey. Those parting words by our facilitator gave each of us that evening both comfort and hope.

The father's bereavement group I meet with are not the only
grief support groups I have sought out and participated in; but I
know that without the support provided by such groups, sharing
with other grieving parents, and especially sharing with other grieving fathers, I would never have been able to reach the point of getting
better because I could never have gotten here alone.

A friend loves at all times, and a brother is
born for a difficult time. (Proverbs 17:17 CSB)

Chapter 8

May

Every good thing and every perfect gift is from above,
coming down from the father of lights, with whom
there is no variation, or shifting shadow.
—James 1:17 NASB

When I was growing up, the month of May was a very special month of the year for me that I always looked forward to living through. For starters, both my birthday and Mother's Day occur during the month of May, and once every so many years or so, both events would fall on the same date. I fondly recall those combined special days when I got to share my birthday with my mother on Mother's Day as being my most memorable childhood birthdays. May was also the month to enjoy the pleasant weather that sunny Southern California was blessed to have; and of course, I got to play Little League baseball games twice a week with my brother and many of my childhood buddies who were often my teammates, and my dad who was usually our coach. Later as a college student, my final exams always interfered with most of my birthday celebrations, but I still did not let that tarnish my enthusiasm for the month of May. Of course, I always looked forward both as a student and then later as an educator to the counting down of the days to the end of the school year in June.

But above all, just when I thought nothing could make my love for the month of May take on an even bigger dynamic than it already did, it got better. On May 28, 1997, God blessed my wife, Kirsti, and me with a second gift from heaven with the birth of our younger son, Nicholas David Contreras. With Nick's birth, my wife and I came to the belief that our family was now perfect and complete.

As parents, we all treasure memories of the births of each of our children as well as cherish the moment we first lay eyes upon each one of them. Those memories will always be on equal terms with all the happiest days of our lives. But for all of us grieving parents, what once brought smiles and joy to our hearts every time we recalled the day we welcomed our late son or daughter into this world now changes when they go to heaven before you. That remembrance of that beautiful day is now accompanied by tears and sorrow as we also recall the sad day that they physically left this world and us.

Ever since my son Nick died, the month of May has lost much of the luster that once brought me such fun and joy as a child and even more so when I remember how much happiness it brought to Nick and the way his enthusiasm would spread to our family and his friends. Now I watch as my wife only takes in half the joy of Mother's Day that she used to because she knows the other half of what made it such a great day for her is now gone. And I admit, on occasion, to having gone through a hard time while trying to enjoy my own birthday because I miss how much fun Nick could make it for me. And even now, the end of the month of May can still bring unknown and unpredictable emotions in me as we mark another year that Nick won't get to be the star of the day, for he so enjoyed celebrating his own birthday.

After Nick's passing, the month of May no longer felt the same as it brought on so many reminders of what should have been rites of passage for Nick. The approach I took toward May now found me wishing I could hide away or take a thirty-one-day nap, hoping it would all be gone when I woke up so that I wouldn't have to feel the pain for what Nick was missing and for what I was missing. But aside from the birthdays and Mother's Days that my wife and I attempted to keep low key in order to ease our pain, it was my profession that wouldn't fully allow me to escape those month of May moments that I felt cheated out of.

As a high school teacher and an athletic director, I was unable to ignore completely all that Nick would have taken part in. He died the winter before he would have entered high school; and many of the experiences he looked forward to and would have enjoyed—had he been given the chance—always seemed to affect me emotionally as I was confronted by that fact every year come May. Needless to say, in the last ten years of my professional career prior to my retirement, the month of May no longer lived up to what I had treasured as a kid or as a father prior to Nick having passed away.

Right by our house, there is a beautiful neighborhood public park that over the years has become a favorite location to take pictures prior to formal school dances for the students of the local high school that Nick would have attended. Every May before the prom, the park is inundated with teenagers and their parents as the boys are handsomely dressed in their tuxedos and the girls are beautifully dressed in their formal gowns as they all look so grown-up. I remember, for four years after Nick had died, dreading that moment that I would be driving by the park and catching a glimpse of his friends and their prom dates. Well, that moment did come, and all I wanted to do was cry.

I remembered as I drove slowly past the park wondering if they were possibly thinking of or holding a place in their hearts in remembrance of their friend, my son Nick, who was noticeably absent from such a memorable high school event. And even if I had chosen to ignore what was going on at the park by my house, I could still not escape it. The reason I could not ignore it was because for ten years after Nick died, I still had to live through every end-of-the-year senior moment at my own school as my students also went through their excited anticipation of their own prom experiences and end-of-the-year senior festivities.

Besides the prom night, I still had to go through other middle-to end-of-May school events that could just as easily stir a trigger in me. Because of my other responsibilities on campus, I still had to take part in such events as the annual spring sports banquets, which

I was directly responsible for putting together; and I often had to take part in the senior awards night program as well. But the one emotional event that always seemed to get to me during those last ten years before retirement was the graduation ceremonies for which I was required to attend as a faculty member.

During the first four graduation ceremonies that occurred before Nick would have had his own high school graduation, I remember feeling a sense of anxiety. This no doubt occurred because of what I knew to be the eventuality that I would have to face the day that would have been his own graduation. And even after Nick's class graduated, I still felt emotional during those graduations that followed because they often brought on in me to a sense of envy for what he; my wife, Kirsti; and me never got to experience with him as his proud parents.

Graduation was always going to be a tricky situation because our home is less than a mile from the high school Nick would have attended, and it was within a legible hearing distance of any major event such as the graduation ceremonies itself. I wasn't always home on the date of the local high school graduation, and after Nick died, if I was home, my wife and I would be sure to go out to dinner or a movie so that we could avoid hearing the ceremony taking place and seeing the line of traffic of the graduates and their families making their way through the neighborhood, heading toward whatever celebrations they had planned. And on the actual day that my son Nick would have graduated from his high school, I was provided with a mixed blessing of sorts because, as it just so happened, my own school was having their own graduation ceremony as well.

Had Nick been alive to graduate from high school, I would have been given permission to miss my own schools ceremony that year as it had been a long-standing courtesy for any staff member, whose son or daughter was graduating on the same day from another high school, to be excused from attending. I am sure if I had asked, I probably could have gotten permission to miss my school's ceremony that year from my boss, who was very much aware of the significance of that particular day for me. But as it turns out, despite the emotions going through me on that day, I preferred to be at my school's graduation instead of being at home and having to hear the ceremony over the loudspeakers reminding me that Nick should have been graduating at that very ceremony too.

That day at school was a long one for me. And even though I held it together and showed no outward emotion, I felt inclined to send an email to staff members that morning who had been there long enough to know of my circumstances and/or who definitely knew Nick. I let them know that "today would also have been my son Nick's high school graduation." I quoted some lyrics from the Kenny Loggins song, "House at Pooh Corner," because Winnie the Pooh was a favorite of my son Nick's, and I wanted to thank everyone for their support over the past four years.

Thinking back, there have been times that I have questioned whether I should have sent the email at all. Did I do it because I wanted to do my son justice and remind those who did know him that I did not want him to be forgotten? Did I want those I worked with to know that this was supposed to be his big day too? Did I do it to run interference for myself in case I did have an emotional breakdown? Did I need to remind people that my son was a very special kid and those who remembered him were welcome to say his name to me? Or did I do it because of what I had been going through for the past four years and what I was still going through on that day? Did I feel the need to let everyone know that I wasn't as tough as many perceived that I may have been, and I really needed some sympathetic nods or a thoughtful pat on the back that might be necessary for me get through the day? In looking back, I believe the answer to all those questions was *yes*.

I will tell you that I did survive, and I made it through that day. I remember receiving a few nice and touching responses to my email—mostly from those who once knew Nick such as my boss and some of the ladies who had always been supportive of me—and I was very thankful for that. And I did manage to get through the graduation ceremony without any noticeable emotions that others would have picked up on, but it wasn't easy because I did have Nick on my mind throughout the entire graduation. After the ceremony was over, I admit to successfully avoiding the celebrating crowds of kids and their parents, and I went to dinner as I always have done after each graduation ceremony with some of my closest colleagues.

At dinner, we all celebrated the end of another year and shared our good, bad, and often funny experiences of the school year that had just ended; and we shared what our plans were for the summer break. And the good friends that they all are, we toasted to the memory of my son Nick. When dinner was over, we said our goodbyes, wished each other a well-deserved summer break, and then I drove myself about halfway home. At some point on the road driving back to my hometown, I had to pull over because I needed to stop crying.

As the years have passed by, the month of May that I loved and remembered as a kid and before my son Nick died has never truly returned. Not that over the years I have not had any pleasant memories on any given day in May, but it never escapes me that at the end of each May there is always the day that we would have celebrated Nick's birthday. I never know how I am going to react at the end of May. I admit to having had moments of sadness for what should be or should have been, but I have also experienced happiness recalling some of his or even my own birthday's past. I also have come to accept that the uneasy butterflies I get in my stomach still feel the same regardless if I am experiencing a sad or happy memory, and the tears I shed be they internally or externally are an annual given reaction whether or not I share them with my family and friends. But the one thing I can always count on is the memory of the first birthday Nick was in heaven. On that day, God provided us a miracle moment that still brings my wife and me comfort and the belief that God is with us and that heaven exists.

On that day, as many of us gathered in the cul-de-sac outside our home on a cloudy day that had followed an unseasonably pretty good rainfall, we released balloons that we had written messages on for Nick. As we released them, a hole in the clouds opened up, revealing a patch of blue in the otherwise dark sky. The balloons we released then all seemingly funneled themselves through the blue hole upward toward heaven, delivering my son his messaged birthday balloons. That moment confirmed my belief in God and heaven, and it is forever branded in my mind. And I have always loved that when that miracle moment happened, I just knew that God had given to Nick the opportunity to once again be the star of his biggest and most favorite day in May.

Every year, the month of May comes and goes, and my emotions are all over the place. But the memory of that miracle moment we experienced that first birthday without Nick can bring me both joy and comfort in knowing that he is okay, and it reminds me of where he is. It has been almost twelve years since that miracle moment, and when I remember Nick's first birthday in heaven, I can now feel free to smile before I cry without any guilt. I don't have to give up on the entire month anymore because as time progresses, I see the very real chance that the month of May might find its way back into the heart of this forever grieving father.

> Here is the message we have heard from Christ and now announce to you: God is light, and in him there is no darkness at all. (1 John 1:5 ESV)

Chapter 9

June

You make known to me the path of life; you will fill me with joy
in your presence, with eternal pleasures at your right hand.
—Psalm 16:11

For many who get through the month of June, it marks when you have passed the midpoint of the traditional calendar year, but for me, getting through June also marks the midpoint of another year without Nick. The month of June will continue me on or redirect me on an uncertain road map with God as my tour guide as he leads me forward to the end of another year in my grief.

Depending on how the first half of the year in my journey of grief has progressed, June can also become the transitional month that allows me to reflect on the past and look forward to a more hopeful future. But early in my grief, with the end of the school year bringing before me the sight of my students looking forward to their own summer breaks, my reflections too often brought to the surface deep thoughts associated with the what once was, what could have been, and what should have been. It is at those times that guilt also set in for me, and it tested my heart and my faith, leading me to at times to question any possible positive progression that I may have been making in my grief.

For years, June traditionally marked when I exhaled from a busy year of teaching and/or coaching high schoolers both in the classroom and on the football and baseball fields and making plans and time to do more with my family. My summer plans were to include time for physical and emotional rest, fun and exciting vacations with my family, the occasional feasting on backyard BBQs, and daily frolicking with my family in our swimming pool, all while creating happy family memories to one day look back upon with fondness. Yes, every June, my intended goal was to enjoy my summer break, be with my family, be free from school and the responsibilities I was often charged with on campus, and returning refreshed for a new school year. But it didn't always work out as planned.

Many of us have jobs and careers that often demand extra time outside the regular work day or work week, and my job as I saw it was no different. When I was coaching, I felt obligated to provide my student-athletes with preseason conditioning workouts; and as an athletic director, I felt I needed to make myself available to my coaches, administrators, parents, and the vendors we did business with. And this meant going into school at least three days a week even if it was only during the early morning to lunchtime hours. I admit to both willingly and at times unwillingly falling victim to the secular world's definition of what it takes to be a success. In hindsight, what I found was that when we men spend that kind of time engulfed in our secular working world, those who lose out due to our absence are going to be our family, meaning our wives and our children.

I wish I could say that my failure to fulfill my intended summer breaks with my family were the combined fault of my jobs and their demands and to myself due to my dedication to my work and my sense of responsibility that I felt my duties entailed. In further hindsight, it seems that my attempts to dole out partial blame to the work world we live in would not be fair despite the reality of it because ultimately it was my choice.

Over the years prior to my retirement from education, the positions I held at the school and district I was employed at were as a history teacher, football and baseball coach, and as an athletic director, and none of them officially required me to work during the summer. None of the duties I performed outside of the school year were actually in my job descriptions as spelled out in my contract. I was not even paid for the time I put in between June and mid-August. That was my choice, and therefore, I do not believe it would be right to spread the blame.

In my last school of employment from which I retired, I was rarely, if ever, "officially" commended for going in on my own time. And to be fair, had I chosen not to come in, no one would have *officially* reprimanded me for not doing so. Though it was not my intent, there was no professional gain to be made, such as promotions, by my choosing to come in on my own time. And as I accept the bulk of the blame for missing out on family time because I put too much emphasis on my professional career, the burden of guilt always has a place in my thoughts.

I do not bring up my work ethic and perceived importance of my former jobs in order to brag, but I do so because I want to share how painfully it reminds me of all the missed time with my boys that I will never get back. And when you add into the equation the losing of one of your children as I did, there will be times when all I can think of are the moments I missed with my son Nick. It kills me emotionally to think of what I missed with not just my late son Nick but also his brother JP. I think of how they may have felt during our summer breaks, waking up in the morning with plans for a shared day with their dad only to find that, just like during the regular school year, I was not home because I had already left for school before they both woke up.

Despite all my best intentions for the month of June, over the years I have often looked back and felt so much regret and guilt for the times I chose to put my work ahead of spending more time with my family when I didn't need to. In recent years, especially since my retirement, I have been doing my best to make amends with my older son, JP, by spending time with him and his wife and my grandson, but it breaks my heart still that I cannot do the same for Nick. And the "what could have been" and "what should have been" thoughts can still haunt me, whether I think about them, talk about them, or write about them. They can still bring tears to my eyes.

Sometimes it feels as though I spend a lot of time writing in my personal journal to Nick during the during the month of June, and though the following closing to an entry is not exclusive to just the month of June, I sometimes feel its impact more in June than in other months.

> Daddy is so sorry son. I am so sorry if and when I hurt your feelings, made you feel sad, or I disappointed you. Please forgive me. I am so sorry. You are the best thirteen-year-old boy in the whole wide world. Your daddy loves you.

Chapter 10

What Could Have Been, What Should Have Been

No, dear brothers and sisters, I have not achieved
it, but I focus on this one thing: Forgetting the
past and looking forward to what lies ahead.
—Philippians 3:13 NLT

Over the years throughout my grief journey, the scriptures have been of tremendous help to me in easing the emotional pain brought on by my son's passing away. For example, reading Matthew 5:4 comforts me, knowing God loves me as I grieve, and when reading Psalm 147:3, I do feel assured that God heals my wounds from the pain of my loss. During the times when my spirit feels crushed, I can look to Psalm 34:18 and feel God's empathy and closeness toward me, and in Revelations 21, God assures me of heaven's existence and the knowledge of where my son Nick is and that our reunion in heaven will be a happy and joyous one.

In GriefShare, I learned that we never "move on" because that would mean leaving what we love behind. As a participant and later as a facilitator, I have always encouraged the preferred phrases of "progressing" or "moving forward" because they allude to us taking with us those and that which we love, and in the case of a grieving parent, that would be our child. So you can imagine the confusion

I am confronted with whenever scripture encourages leaving behind and looking forward. During those moments when grief has taken over the front seat and steers our present thoughts, we are not in the right frame of mind to try and truly dig deep into scriptures that seemingly encourage us to leave painful memories behind.

When we look back into our past, it is the memories of our child that usually dominate our thoughts, and the idea of forgetting or leaving them behind is a worst-case scenario that we have always feared in our minds. And when fishing through the Bible to look for scripture to relieve our sorrows, there is always the possibility that we may easily take out of context the meaning of the full lesson of chapters and verses we come upon. What we may fixate on are the partial verses of the books and chapters while not considering the before and after explanations that will make clearer what God intends for us to learn from it. In doing so, we find ourselves confused by what seems to be contradictory lessons to what we may have come to understand as part of our healing process throughout our journey.

On the surface, 2 Corinthians 5:17 looks like it is reminding you that the past is the past, and it is time to look forward to the new. But as a grieving parent, even if we understand the spiritual and emotional meaning of moving forward, no one wants to be told to move on toward something new without at least a subtle reminder or even encouragement to take their deceased child with them. And in Ecclesiastes 7:10, there is confusion as to why the scripture would question, "Why are former days better than these?" Because as grieving parents, in our minds the better days were indeed before the present days when our child was still with us here on earth.

This, of course, may lead you, the reader, to wonder why I opened up this chapter with Philippians 3:13. After all, this scripture verse seems to be out of place when you have read that I believe I will always take my son with me, both in my heart and in my everyday thoughts. But what I have found is that it is not my worst-case scenario that God has in mind when he brings these scriptures before me; if anything, he is reinforcing what brings me comfort and purpose for all concerned, and that includes my son Nick in heaven.

I was playing catch with my grandson recently out in our cul-de-sac in front of our house when it occurred to me that the last time I had played catch with anyone in front of our house, it was with my son Nick. My grandson had earlier asked about playing catch, so I proceeded to pull down two baseball gloves from the top shelf of our hall closet. One of the gloves was my older son's, JP's, old catchers' mitt, which I chose to use myself, but before I handed over the second glove to my grandson, I hesitated for a slight moment because etched in permanent ink on the side of the glove was clearly marked "Nick C."

After the hesitation had lapsed and I handed the glove over to my grandson, I made sure to show him that the glove had once belonged to his uncle Nick, and he seemed genuinely excited about that. Once we began throwing the ball back and forth, I began to experience some old emotions, reminiscing of days past when I previously would play catch with both my boys, not just Nick. The emotions I felt were not just because of whose glove my grandson was using, but they reminded me of the interaction I would have with my sons when we participated in this activity.

You see, it didn't take very long for me to go into my coaching mode and begin instructing my grandson on the finer arts of how to catch a ball and how to step and throw. I immediately began to see that it didn't take long for him to get frustrated by my constant interrupting of our "game of playing catch" to coach him. I could only guess from the look on his face that soon to follow would be his telling me, "Grandpa, I don't want to play anymore. Can we do something else?"

I had seen that look on his face and heard that phrase before as it was the same ones both of my sons would make and say when they were little, and I proceeded to coach them instead of playing with them. Coming back to me in my mind were the guilt-filled memories of how I ruined some potentially fond father-son moments because I was trying to coach them, when all they really wanted to do was to just play catch with their dad. I reminded myself that it was years too late for me to do anything about it with my sons Nick and JP but not so for my grandson.

Within a short time of realizing I had taken my coaching persona out of retirement, I immediately returned it back to its place and replaced it with my, hopefully, more jovial grandpa self, and we ended up having a pleasant time just "playing catch." And I let my grandson talk his heart out as we just had fun.

Later that evening, after my grandson went home with his parents and I was sitting at my computer recording my thoughts for the day, my memories began to move into old familiar territories that a grieving father often floats into when the possibility of past regrets and/or guilt feelings sets in. The thoughts of the "what I could have done" or "should have done" with my son Nick came pouring in, bringing me to the brink of tears. I can never quite guess how I will react to my recollections of the times when Nick would approach me and ask me, "Dad, can we do this or that?" or "Dad, would you like to do this or that with me?" and how during some of those times I may have disappointed him when the answers were not yes. And on this particular evening, they did bring back some feelings of guilt and regret.

What returned to me were the questions I ask less and less as the years go by but that I occasionally do return to. I will ask myself if I failed him during his lifetime, and I wonder what his opinions of his dad were when he died. Yes, my work schedule often did not give me the time I would have liked to have had to fulfill his wishes, and to my wife's credit and with my complete support, Kirsti often filled his free time from school with swim or water polo practices and contests, art classes, music lessons, Lego camps, church youth ministries, and spring and summer camps and activities. But even with all those meaningful, fun, spiritual, and enriching activities that he so enjoyed participating in, I still wonder if I failed in giving him that something he may have wanted just as much, if not more—that being, spending time with me, his dad. I do know that I wish I had done so.

It hurts me to bring up memories of times when I feel that I failed my son when he was here, but please, I don't want to give you the impression that I spent or gave very little or no time with my son Nick or his brother, JP, for that matter. I do not want you to think that I did not support his activities and/or interests, but I do want you to recognize that I too have those moments in the process of my grief while missing my son when I lament on what I could have or should have done to make his life happier. Like any other grieving father in my position, I shouldn't beat myself up so bad that I forget that I really did do my best to make his life happy when he was here, and above all, I need to remember that while he was here, he made me extremely happy and proud to be his dad. All he ever had to do for me to feel happy was at the end of his day just to say to me the words, "I love you, Dad!"

Nick was so naturally skilled at so many things and so creative with his imagination that I often went between being proud and in awe at how his mind worked and, at other times, fearing the inevitable day that he would find out his dad had limitations and that he may not need me anymore.

When Nick was about ten years old, he had it in his mind that we could build a small playhouse in the backyard. He even drew up some impressive plans for it. He was going to use materials we had lying around the house and in the garage, and I recall a few times him telling me that we should go out the next morning or today and get going on it. It was summer, and it was boiling hot. And I was able to get out of it by inviting his friends over to spend the day playing in our swimming pool—a pastime he enjoyed more than anything because he loved being with his friends. Though later he never mentioned if he was disappointed at not building the playhouse, I still feel hurt sometimes thinking I should have at least tried it with him.

What Nick never realized was that my reluctance to build the playhouse with him was my fear that he would realize his dad was not who he may have thought I was. When I think back on it, I guess I should feel flattered that my son thought of me as the person he wanted to help him and that doing this project was going to be a father-son thing he wanted us to do together. I have never had those types of skills, and I truly feared while my boys were growing up that I would drop a notch in their eyes because of what I couldn't do. JP is okay with it now that he knows or understands his dad's limits, and we even laugh about what I can help him with and what he would rather do by himself. But Nick? It still hurts because I will never know what he thought of what his dad was good at or not or what I made him proud of or not. Now I wish I had shared more, done more, and tried more. Perhaps he would have taught me more.

I am sure I could make a long list of all the "what I could have done or should have done," and in the process, we could flip a coin to decide who likes me less, you the reader or me the writer. And any grieving father out there who is also going through or has gone through these thoughts may feel the same. But I think it is important before we go down the rabbit hole of regret and depression over what was or what should have been, we need to separate into two imaginary piles the lists of good and happy from the bad and sad. If you are like me because our child is in heaven and we miss them, the sad and bad pile seems to make the most impact when remembering our initial grief, which causes most of our tears and sorrows because of the pain of reliving their death and the missing of their presence with us. But what takes varying amounts of time in our journey of grief is the realization that in comparison, the size and impact of the pile of good and happy are far more significant and numerous than anything the sad and bad can throw at us.

As time goes by and my journey of grief continues on, I will always take my son Nick's memory with me, never leaving him behind. But part of doing so means that I will bring with me baggage that will include the occasional feelings of guilt and hurt about what could have been and should have been. For example, I have felt sadness at the thought that my handsome thirteen-year-old son may have never known what it was like to go on a date, hold hands with, or kiss a girl. But I do remember once when I picked him up from midweek youth service at our church that he was so excited to tell me that he had a girlfriend. They had a mutual breakup two weeks later, but any sadness I have on thinking back to that time ends in happy tears when I think of how he wanted to share that moment with me, his dad.

If my guilt feelings about not building the playhouse with Nick would haunt me because I feared his disappointment in me, all I have to do is remember that I was Nick's cabin counselor at his church summer camps. For three summers, I could see in his eyes how proud he was of me being the cabin leader and how much more fun his cabin was and how his cabinmates felt lucky that they were with Nick's dad. (I guess being an experienced schoolteacher and coach may have helped.) And I got to see a side of Nick I never got to see at home as he shared in fellowship with his friends, shared in the Bible lessons, being a leader, and being a young brother in Christ. Then there was the pride we both felt when, at the age of eleven, he chose to be baptized in the lake on the last day of one of the summer camps.

With my wife, Kirsti, having driven up the mountain to be a witness among the crowd, I, along with the camp pastor, stepped into the lake with Nick; and we both helped him to immerse himself under the water as Nick accepted Jesus Christ as his Lord and Savior, creating a moment between father and son that more than made up for any missed moment I still wish I had done with him. God gave that baptismal moment to both of us, and it will never leave my mind, and it will always be burnt permanently in my heart as one of my most cherished moments as an earthly father.

As for the day when my grandson and I played catch and how it started my thoughts on writing this chapter and dealing with the guilt for what should have been or could have been, I remember as I was making my way to bed that evening, all I could think of was that last time I played catch with Nick. He hadn't played organized baseball for a couple of years, and out of nowhere, he just came to me one day and said, "Dad, let's go outside and play catch!" I remember being surprised because our last encounter with baseball together led him to decide he no longer wished to play anymore. But what I remember was that, as we went out to the cul-de-sac, pretty much in the same spot where I played with my grandson years later, Nick and I got into a real good groove. I was surprised how well he could still catch and throw a baseball. His throws were strong and accurate, likely the result of his cross-training by throwing a bigger and heavier water polo ball in the swimming pool, but what really caught my attention was that I had no thought of coaching him at all. I don't even remember if I mentioned how well he was catching or throwing the ball. All I know is that we were just simply playing catch and having a wonderful father-and-son chat.

I do remember that most of the talking between us was being done by Nick, and I was enjoying listening to him, and to this day, I can still recall the sound of his voice. I remember him telling me of his latest adventures at school, how his favorite class in school was woodshop, and how he described some of the characters in the books he was reading. I remember thinking how creative he was as he explained to me some of his ideas for his newest Lego creations, and he made me laugh about some of the funny scenes from his favorite television show, *The Big Bang Theory.*

At the time, I didn't think of that moment in emotional terms as I do today; but now whenever I think of that day, I can be moved to tears, but the tears are not sad ones. If I do experience any shades of sadness for that moment, it is likely the result of my wishing that I had done that with him more often. I truly wished I had been more aware that my son didn't want to "practice baseball with a coach." He just wanted to "play catch with his dad." But the tears of wishing I had more of those moments have never been greater than the happy memory that I did have that one moment between us that I now cherish to no end.

Any emotional pain I may now feel whenever I relive those types of moments is less in severity as I now use them to help bridge my past to my present regarding my son and any thoughts of guilt that still lay inside of me. And I now consider that perhaps Philippians 3:13 is not telling me to "forget the past"; instead, it encourages me to live in the present by doing God's will today for tomorrow. I believe that my moment of playing catch with my son Nick before he died was meant by God to one day be a teachable moment for me as I continue moving forward in my spiritual journey as well as my grief journey.

As I was playing catch with my grandson on the very same spot as the last time I did so with his uncle years before, I felt as though God was allowing me to receive a message from my son Nick. To me, the message was very clear as I could hear my son speaking to me, and I could hear the sound of his voice as he was saying to me, "Thanks, Dad, for playing catch with me."

> Don't copy the behavior and customs of this world, but let God transform you into a new person by changing the way you think. Then you will learn to know God's will for you, which is good and pleasing and perfect. (Romans 12:2 *NLT)*

Chapter 11

July Transition

May the God of hope fill you with all joy and peace in believing,
so that by the power of the Holy Spirit you may abound in hope.
                                          —Romans 15:13 ESV

For years, the month of July has represented a part of the year when I am free from all that the pressures and issues that the secular world can place before me, and it allows me the freedom to not obsess about the remaining year to come or to lament over the first half of the year I have just left behind. True, when I was still working, my job never really completely went away for a true summer break, and even though I am now retired, it has not put an end to my grief. But what July has always provided me both then and now is a buffer between the first half of the year where I live with what seems to be constant reminders that can trigger my emotions and the remaining half of the year, which often seems unpredictable as to how I will emotionally complete it.

I also feel that, since Nick died, the month of July has provided me with some much-needed moments of peace from what at times can feel like a constant barrage of emotions in my heart. It allows me to embrace the comfort provided by God as he reminds me that it is okay to smile, laugh, and love all that he has blessed me with in my life, and that includes my late son Nick. And though God has also brought before me many additional challenges that have affected my family and that may have added to my already emotional plate, in hindsight I can see that they did not replace nor lessen my grief. As a matter of fact, some of those July challenges placed before me have made my need to grieve for my son stronger under a transitional mode in which to reflect the good, the happiness, and the love I will always hold for my son that coincides with the same love and emotions I continue to hold for my family and loved ones who are with me still here on earth.

That first July after Nick passed away, I experienced how his death and my ensuing grief would affect and permanently establish the priorities of my family's needs over my own. It became more evident to me then and has continued to do so now even more what are God's plans for me and how he was shaping the path my life would follow from then on.

A couple of months into my first summer break from school after Nick passed away, I found myself in the position of having to make a major decision that would affect the rest of my professional career. I had applied for two identical positions at a local two-high-school district near the one I was employed at. What at first looked to be a promising opportunity, I later instead found myself withdrawing at the last minute from both of the administrative positions that I had interviewed for and was a finalist.

In GriefShare, we learn that in the first year of grief, it is wise not to make major decisions that will affect your life if it can be helped. Selling your house and moving away or getting married or making major financial investments are examples, and the one that applied to me was the one that cautioned you about changing jobs or careers. Yes, I was aware of the last recommendation, but prior to my son's passing, I was actively looking for the type of career move that had suddenly become available just six months after my son Nick went to heaven. After careful thought and discussion with my wife, I convinced myself that a change in work locations may actually be a good thing for me, so I applied for both the identical positions at the two-high-school district.

From what I was told later by others who were familiar with the schools involved, I did well in the interview process, and I was one of the top two candidates who would likely have been offered one of the two positions. But the numerous combinations of the closeness to the time when Nick had passed away—the emotional needs of both my wife, Kirsti, and my older son, JP; my working even further away from home; and the thought of leaving the emotional support I was receiving from those at my own school—all led me to the decision that it was not the right time to begin a new job in a different location.

As it turned out, I did not realize at the time that my decision to withdraw was to be my last true opportunity for advancement in my career in education. In hindsight, I now see that God knew where it was I needed to be, both for myself and for my family. It so happened a couple of days after withdrawing from consideration from either of the two positions that I was being considered for, we found out that my wife, Kirsti, was diagnosed with a rare and aggressive form of cervical cancer.

Needless to say, upon learning of my wife's cancer diagnosis, concern for her health now took on an equal priority alongside our still-fresh grief for our son Nick. From that moment on, any career goals or ambitions that I may still have had lingering in me after my son Nick's passing away were to be permanently impacted by the challenges of not only the loss of our son but also the very real danger of her cancer. This second blow to our family, within six months after losing Nick, would shape the remainder of my working career as it forever placed any career goals below those of the emotional and physical needs of my family.

The culmination of all these events during that trying time and the years that have followed since have brought me to the realization that July truly does fit in as the transitional month in the yearly journey of my life and grief. I now can reflect on what was truly important in my past and what can truly be happy days ahead. I can reinforce my need to move forward in my grief progression, and together with my family, we could take both new and old approaches in our lives to learn that we can once again laugh, love, and create new memories. And more importantly, we can establish ourselves in what is now our new normal.

You who have made me see many troubles and calamities will revive me again; from the depths of the earth you will bring me up again. You will increase my greatness and comfort me again. (Psalm 71:20–21 ESV)

Chapter 12

Vacations and Nick's Presence

I pray that the God who gives hope will fill you with
much joy and peace while you trust in him. Then your
hope will overflow by the power of the Holy Spirit.
—Romans 15:13

Before Nick died, July was the month that we usually made time for many of the family activities and experiences that we would later hold so dear for our summer family memories. July provided us with so many opportunities to enjoy such things as family vacations, neighborhood Fourth of July block parties, BBQs in our backyard, and all-day swimming in our pool. And even though the blistering Sacramento summer heat would beat down on me during an all-day Saturday swim meet, I absolutely loved watching my boys compete in the pool. But by far, the most memorable July experiences we shared as a family were our numerous summer vacations in Hawaii.

For Kirsti and me, our happiest summertime memories and joys were centered around what came to be our every other year visits to the Big Island. We had visited that island before we had kids, and we did our best to visit as often as we could once we had the boys. The Big Island has become like a second home in our hearts due to our familiarity with it and the fact that our boys grew up enjoying some of their summer vacations there.

The happy recollections of our vacations in Hawaii are full of our family enjoying the snorkeling, kayaking, paddle boarding, and hiking activities that made for a lifetime of cherished memories for all of us. With pride, I can still see both my boys who were both strong and confident swimmers, experiencing once-in-a-lifetime water adventures such as swimming with the dolphins and turtles and nighttime swimming with the manta rays. They got to behold sights that few ever get to witness in their lifetimes such as seeing lava seeping out of the ground literally yards beyond their feet and hiking a hardened lava field to a point where they got to see lava flowing into the sea at the Volcano National Park.

We also grew to love the humorous side of our vacations such as once during a *luau*, as they were moving the cooked pig out of the pit to lay on display for all to see, the head broke off and rolled on the ground. Many of the people that were there were horrified by the sight of the pigs rolling head, but not my Nick. He laughed uncontrollably, and I am sure if he could have had his way, he would have asked them do it again.

JP and Nick loved our vacations in Hawaii. They easily loved adapting to island life, and I so admired how they both could so easily make friends, whether it was at the pool at the resort with other tourist kids or on the sandy beaches with some of the locals. They seemed to be able to feel at home. And their positive experiences in Hawaii were not exclusively limited to only the Big Island as they both had created for themselves fond memories of some of the other islands they visited as well. For example, it was on Kauai they learned to body- and stand-up surf on the waves, and once when we were on Oahu, we experienced another one of our more amusing moments when, after visiting the USS *Arizona* memorial at Pearl Harbor, we observed Nick waving to us from the memorial when he was supposed to be on the boat with us heading back to the pier. And it did cross my mind at the moment that he may have considered jumping into the water and swimming after the boat, but luckily, he decided to wait for the next boat returning to the pier.

The last time we visited Hawaii with Nick was the summer before he passed away. Nick had a wonderful time on that visit, and the pictures show it. Those pictures have become some of the most treasured photographs that we possess. I remember how much Nick enjoyed hanging out with this brother, his mom, and even me, though at times he and I did butt heads because Nick just was starting his rebellious teen years and most often he aimed his teenage rage against me. Despite that, however, I still recall that summer as being one of our most memorable Hawaiian family vacations, but it just never would have crossed my mind that it would be our last one with Nick.

After Nick went to heaven, both Kirsti and I became very reluctant about committing to if and when we wanted to return to Hawaii. We just didn't know how to incorporate happiness into our new normal, especially into our happy place without Nick.

Because our vacations often provided some of our most cherished moments as a family, it is easy to understand how painful it was for us to consider visiting any of our familiar vacation haunts or even new ones with the knowledge that Nick would not be joining us. With few exceptions, we did not venture far from our home that first year after Nick passed away, and if we did, there was a lot of inner struggles for us to feel any joy or comfort that could match any of our previous vacations that now did not include him.

There were a few exceptions, and one of those was a trip that Kirsti, JP, and I took to Costa Rica after the school year was out. This was a trip sponsored by an educational student travel program that originally was to be a trip for Nick, with Kirsti going along as a chaperone. They had both been looking forward to it, but when Nick died, we found ourselves cancelling many of the previously planned trips and activities that were to be participated in by Nick. The woman in charge of the Costa Rica trip, however, had been one of Nick's teachers, and she encouraged Kirsti and me to go along with JP as a tribute to Nick's memory.

At the time, all three of us felt like it was the right thing to do, and perhaps in another time and under different circumstances, I am sure that it would have been a much more memorable and pleasurable experience than it turned out to be. But the closeness in proximity to the time of Nick's passing made it impossible not to keep him in our every moment's thoughts. But as difficult as it was, it still had its good moments, and I later came to realize that it was possible to have Nick be with us on such a trip, even if only in in spirit.

Costa Rica was beautiful. It was adventurous, and it was just the type of trip that Nick would have enjoyed. On that trip, we were fortunate to have attending with us both parents and kids who knew Nick. Of those who attended and knew Nick well were his best friend and his mother who was also a chaperone. Her presence was of great comfort for both Kirsti and me when our emotional moments were triggered. There was also a young girl who was a teammate of Nick from the swim team and whose mother knew Nick, JP, and Kirsti. Also travelling with us was a friend of Nick from church whose own adventurous and free-spirited ways reminded us daily of our Nick throughout the trip. And of course, there were so many exotic animals, from the monkeys, sloths, alligators, as well as the many varieties of birds, snakes, frogs, lizards, and bugs—all of which would have made Nick excited beyond belief.

To be honest, every time an occasion arose to observe the animal wildlife, my exact thoughts always turned to Nick as I tried to fight, often unsuccessfully, through the tears. So often did Nick enter my mind as I watched the sights in Costa Rica that my most often used comment that I shared with my wife, Kirsti, was, "Nick would have loved this." So beautiful were the many different species of animals seen and the sights we viewed that I am fairly sure that when we returned home, Nick would have been anxious to draw and then paint them on canvas.

Another time that I was able to share a moment with Nick occurred ironically when we attended, along with all the kids and chaperones on the trip, the opening of the last *Harry Potter* movie. Both of my boys were big *Harry Potter* fans, having seen the movies and read the books, and Nick had been looking forward to the final movie. I knew it was going to be very emotional for me to see it without Nick, but I had been planning to make sure that Nick would see that last *Harry Potter* with me as we had always planned to do. While sitting in the theatre, I took out my wallet and opened it up to his picture, and I placed it in the cupholder next to my seat, facing the big screen. I was determined to make sure that we saw that movie together. So for a few hours in an English-speaking movie theatre in Costa Rica of all places, we did exactly that, with me sitting next to my opened wallet with Nick's picture facing the movie screen. When the movie was over, I swear I could hear him say just as he did at the very first movie of the series, "Yay, Harry Potter!"

Upon returning home from that trip, I had some mixed emotions as I admittedly felt a sense of welcomed relief. I was never able to truly and completely let loose and feel relaxed, constantly fighting off the triggers that had me on an emotional roller coaster and constantly thinking of and missing my son Nick. But later, when I looked back on that trip, it helped me to understand the premise of moving forward without Nick's physical presence with me on earth, and I also learned to understand how it could and would be possible in the future to always take Nick with me in my heart anywhere I go. This I have done every day since, and I will continue to do so while I am still here.

As I had mentioned before at the beginning of this chapter, Julys were traditionally our prime vacation month. But on some occasion, our vacations might have taken place in late June or spill into early August. Thanks to my retirement from teaching, my flexibility to take a vacation at any time of the year has allowed Kirsti and me to take advantage of my evermore flexible schedule, which was much more limited when I was still working. But that first July after Nick passed away, we did not go anywhere. Occurrences during that first summer and year for that matter would be very influential in our changing views on going on vacations.

Initially, not wanting to deal with the emotional pain, we did try and stay away from returning to places that had always included Nick. But the combination of passing time, the Costa Rica trip, and Kirsti's battles with cancer allowed us to step forward and accept that, yes, we could take Nick with us in our hearts. And the pain we may have to endure would eventually be turned into tears of happiness for the memories we would and still treasure forever. But it would have to start slowly, a few steps at a time.

With the exception of the Costa Rica trip, we would not make another trip away from home until the following spring, almost thirteen months after Nick had passed away. Even though that next trip would only be over a long weekend, it turned out to be harder than we thought it would be. We had not left our home on a long-distance trip since Costa Rica until it was decided that we would travel down to Southern California to attend my dad's eightieth birthday celebration.

To be honest, I don't recall that I was of any help in the planning for my dad's celebration, mostly because even though it had been thirteen months since my son had died, I still found myself feeling anxious about going back to the last place everyone in my family had last seen Nick alive. I remembered vividly that last family New Year's that we were in Southern California and how Nick was truly coming into his own.

Physically, he was becoming very good-looking, and he was getting taller, having surpassed his brother, JP, in height. And it became evident at the rate he was growing that he would soon be the tallest of all my father's grandchildren. As for his maturity, he was growing in self-confidence. He loved showing off his guitar skills, and he openly challenged his uncle Mark to chess matches every chance that he could. He was noticeably beginning to hold his own socially with his brother and older cousins. I just didn't know if he would be remembered that way, but I do know that it was very important to me that everyone did remember him that way.

The event was supposed to be a celebration for my dad whom we all adore, respect, and love. But in thinking back on it and not that anyone asked me to, there was still a part of me not yet ready to yield the field of attention and empathy from being the grieving father. I do recall that I wasn't looking forward to what emotions might build up inside for having to set aside my open grief, even if only temporarily. But I also knew that I did not want to dampen the evening for my dad and all the hard work my brother Robert and sister Linda put into putting it together. They had no way of knowing that I was still struggling with the realization that some parts of my grief were still fresh thirteen months later and would likely remain so for quite a long time. Add to that was my very real reminder that without Nick, I was having a hard time with the phrase *we* being there because *we* were not all there to celebrate my dad's big night.

I have to think very hard to remember most of what happened that evening. The one thing I do remember for sure is that it rained that evening. It didn't go unnoticed in my mind that perhaps the rain was God doing the crying for me so that I would not have to do so in front of everyone who was there. I can vaguely remember some of my cousins, uncles, and aunts being there and that it was hard to answer the "How are you doing?" or "How have you been?" questions. And I no doubt made them feel uncomfortable when and if my responses to them included my bringing up of Nick's passing.

My wife and I were recently reminiscing about that evening, and oddly, we can't recall if our son JP was there. (He did confirm he was there though he can only vaguely remember being there himself.) JP spent much of his time while there with his cousins, and as for Kirsti, she had just recently completed the aggressive chemo and radiation treatments that endured in her first bout with cancer. And she mainly kept company with my sister-in-law Jennifer and other family members who knew us more intimately and also knew of our loss.

As for me, I found it hard to play cohost, but my brother and sister took care of most of that thankfully. The following morning, Kirsti, JP, and I headed back north for home. Thinking back on it, we were glad that we went to the celebration, and we were happy to have been there for my dad, who genuinely loved having all of us there. But honestly, hiding the emotions we had inside of us was draining, and we were relieved to get back home to our safe place, away from having to put on a happy face in lieu of the still lingering sadness that was our grief. It allowed us to return to the freedom to release the tears we had stifled in our eyes during our trip.

Now that I have been a grieving father these past twelve years, I can honestly say to others who may be attempting to offer empathy to a parent of child loss, please do not use the well-meaning but ill-advised cliché, "Time heals all wounds." The passing of time alone will not heal the wound of losing a child; as a matter of fact, the scar remains forever. But there is some truth to the meaning of time when considering how one approaches facing their grief and the accompanying pain in moving forward. As time does go by, I believe that the philosophy of taking baby steps seems to be a far better approach in moving forward with your life during your grief, and it reinforces the truth that each one of us grieves differently.

The truth is that time may not remove all the pain, but over time, it will lessen it. Over time, it will not return you to the lifestyle or normality that was present before your loss, but it will open the opportunities to establish your new normal and to reestablish some old routines if only to remind you of the happiness and gratitude toward God for reminding you of happier times for when your son and/or daughter was still with you.

My family enjoyed vacationing together, be it in July or any other time of the year, and happy memories were made for life. I treasure those memories still and have made no effort whatsoever to forget them, having filed them deep in my thoughts so as not to feel any pain that may come to mind because without Nick, they will never be repeated as I remember them. And because my wife, son JP, and I all needed to grieve our own way in order to accept that whatever each of our new normal would encompass, we would not have to leave him behind from our hearts, but rather, we could always bring him with us.

The time from Nick's passing to our Cost Rica trip to our trip to Southern California to celebrate my father's eightieth birthday did just that. That spring, we took a family trip to Oregon after JP graduated from high school—a trip originally planned with Nick in mind to go as well. We also began what would become our annual trips on or around Nick's angelversary at the beginning of January to San Francisco. The angelversary trips have always included being accompanied every year by my sister Linda and brother-in-law Mark who were not only close to Nick but who have also remained to this day loving sources of support throughout our grief journey for Nick.

Kirsti's three cancer fights have also brought me to the realization of our limitations on earth and that how precious our time together is and should be archived in our hearts for those still here.

This has allowed Kirsti and me to take with us our son Nick as we have renewed our love of travel, and wherever we go, we are comfortable taking him with us if only in our hearts and minds.

After JP's high school graduation, as mentioned before, we vacationed in Oregon on a trip Nick was initially supposed to be on as well—and though I found myself crying alone at times because I was missing him, that trip was so much easier on an emotional scale than Costa Rica and Southern California. Within a year, we found ourselves returning to familiar places like Hawaii, another emotion-filled trip, but what we found was that so many happy memories of Hawaii vacations from our past visits began to outweigh the heartache of Nick's absence. And his spirit was and still is always present with us during each of our return visits to the islands since.

Our annual trips to San Francisco and Southern California have been easier and more enjoyable as they have brought us happy moments and a true sense of Nick's presence among us. But not only have we taken Nick with us when returning to our happy places, but I have also felt his presence on our new adventures and vacations as well. I could feel Nick with me when cruising down the Danube on a river cruise in Europe or attending to family reunions in South Carolina, Ohio, and Indiana, as well as Utah and Colorado. Closer to home in our own home state of California, we have enjoyed family gatherings while making our way back to Lake Tahoe and to the Napa Valley. On each trip, we have experienced at times some pain and sadness. Yes, they do still occur, but we have also learned that we can once again enjoy our trips and somehow know that Nick was with us.

At the writing of this chapter, I am also reminded of two of our most recent family vacations, which included our older son, JP; our daughter-in-law, Kimberly; and our grandson, Nicholai. The first was Hawaii. Because our daughter-in-law and grandson had never been to Hawaii, Kirsti and I found ourselves being touristy again. We both, along with our son JP, wanted them to experience some of the happier events, excursions, and happy experiences we once had that included Nick. Our grandson who seems to want to, at times, embrace the uncle he never knew (he insists on being called "Nick") loved it all, swimming at the resort pool and beaches, horseback riding, snorkeling cruise, hiking, the visit to Volcano National Park, and the luau he and his parents so thoroughly enjoyed. Their presence brought many a happy memory and smile to Kirsti and me. And yes, Nick was with us. I could just feel it. I could see it in the smiles of my family.

The second was a trip to the wintry beauty that was still present when we visited Yosemite National Park. This was a place that Nick never got the chance to visit. My wife and I are embarrassed about that fact because as I was growing up, I visited Yosemite almost as much as I now visit Hawaii, and my wife had visited numerous times including with me. We live in a reasonable proximity to the park, and yet, we had never taken either of our boys. So taking my son JP and his family was a treat for Kirsti and me, and we so loved the beauty of the park, which at that time of year we had only seen in pictures. We also had the opportunity to take our grandson sledding at a snow park just outside the park. The enthusiasm and adventurous way he approached going down the hill reminded me of his uncle Nick who also approached doing so the same way.

Needless to say, we so thoroughly enjoyed being with our family on both vacations, and not once did we feel sadness for Nick not being there. But to the contrary, we smiled often, laughed, and took in the beauty that he no doubt was watching with us from where his home is now. Over the years, I am learning, along with my family, to embrace how good it is to be alive and to share in God's plan and that we are still and always will be a family. I am thankful to God for my family, and that includes his gift of letting Nick enter my heart wherever I go. He has used our new normal so that we may have happy vacations once again.

> You have changed my sorrow into dancing.
> You took away my clothes of sadness, and clothed
> me in happiness. (Psalm 30:11 NCV)

Chapter 13

August

When life is good, enjoy it. But when life is hard,
remember; God gives good times and hard times,
and no one knows what tomorrow will bring.
—Ecclesiastes 7:14 NCV

For former educators like myself, June has traditionally represented the end of the school year, the beginning of summer break,
and the anticipation of fun-filled times to be shared with our families. But just when it seems we are getting used to the well-deserved
rest, relaxation, and freedom from the everyday stress that a school
year brings, our summer comes to an end. But even with all the pos-
itives that a summer break can bring to any hard-working individual,
be it an educator like myself or any other person in the working
world, one thing that is inescapable is our continued grief of a parent
for our sons or daughters.

As I have shared in the previous chapters, during the last ten
years of my working as an educator as well as after my retirement, I
returned to being able to look forward to going on summer vacation
trips with my wife and my family after my son's passing away. But at
the end of every summer came August, and with it was my return to
campus for the new school year to prepare for my classroom and high
school athletic-related responsibilities. But outside of my unpaid visits to my school in August, I would also take time to reflect on my

summer breaks, smiling once again at the pleasant memories of my time spent with my wife, my family, the places we visited, and the adventures we enjoyed. But one thing that my end of summer reflections always revealed about my summer break was that my grief for my son never took a break.

I have always understood that a father's grief does not take time off because grief and its triggers can still occur at any time, and though the emotions we may experience may be less painful over time, they can still stir a lesser form of heartbreak and yearning for the days his family was fully here on earth. Such was the reaction eight years into my grief journey that led me to enter a post in my Facebook group account dedicated to my son Nick that was triggered by a movie called *A River Runs through It* that I watched one summer night.

Below is from the postings in the Nicholas David Contreras Facebook group on August 3, 2019:

> *A River Runs through It*. Has anyone ever seen that movie? The strangest thing happened to me this evening. I had not seen or thought about that movie for a long time. Then tonight, while in church, I was having a hard time concentrating on the pastor's lesson because the movie kept popping into my head.
>
> The movie is about two brothers in Montana who grew up loving to fish in the river with their pastor father. One of them, the younger brother portrayed by a young Brad Pitt, was quite the wild and freestyle adventurer. He was always taking chances, always aiming to catch the biggest fish, and later taking the big chances in life too. The two brothers were loyal to each other. They loved their parents, and their parents loved them. I remember that I liked that movie when it first came out, but I never realized at the time how it would one day have a déjà vu effect to my

own real-life family's story. But as I said before, I am not sure what made me think of that movie tonight, but once again, I am reminded that I am not the same man I was nine years ago.

When Kirsti and I got home from church, she was tired and went to bed, but I went to turn on the television, choosing to stay up a bit and watch some news before I joined her. At the end of the broadcast, as I was about to turn off the television, the opening credits to *A River Runs through It* came on. I remembered the movie and thought how odd it was because I was thinking about this exact movie at church. So I thought I would stay up for a while and watch some of it. But as I began watching it, it dawned on me that this movie was hitting me close to home emotionally because I know how it ends. Despite knowing the ending, I sat back and watched it anyway, knowing very well I would probably watch it till the end.

As the movie progressed, the storyline was touching many of my emotional buttons. I remember thinking to myself, *When this movie is over, I swear I will never watch it again.* But in truth, if given the chance, I probably will watch it again. I will probably watch it because I love seeing the story of the love that a family has for each other and to see their shared love of God. Or perhaps I just needed a reason to cry. But what really magnified me to this movie was the symbol of their love of the river and its impact on their lives. That is what truly got to me and why I sat there till the end.

The water—be it rivers, lakes, oceans, even our backyard pool— brings fond memories for me. You see, my two boys so loved the water.

They enjoyed all the water activities associated with it—be it swimming, surfing, water polo, paddle boarding, snorkeling, or rafting—and JP has even been certified as a scuba diver. So by thinking of the symbolic meaning of the river and all that surrounds it throughout the story in the movie, it hit me harder than I thought it was going to. Then to top it off, of course, the younger brother, played by Brad Pitt, dies toward the end of the movie; and the movie concludes with the elder brother, now a senior citizen, still loving the river, still fishing where he grew up near where he fished with his father and little brother, now handing down his love of the river to his own children and grandchildren.

To me, the river in this movie symbolizes the unbreakable love within a family. It shows me that no matter how long the years go by, our love for each other is like a river. And our love for each other, like the water flowing in it, will go on and on forever. *A River Runs through It*. Yes, I will no doubt watch this movie again someday, preferably alone, so that I may cry in peace. And I will beg the movie to remind me that though Nick is in heaven, he, JP, his mother, and I are still a family, tied together by the symbolic flow of a river that goes on and on forever.

Nick, you are the best thirteen-year-old boy in the whole wide world. Your mommy, daddy, and your big brother JP—all love you, and we always will.

When I posted the above on my Facebook group page, I was not depressed either before or after having done so, but I was feeling emotional. To anyone who may have never experienced grieving for their child, any tears I shed that evening may have come as a surprise to them, wondering how a movie could cause such an impactful trigger on me when it has been over eight years since my son's death, and it might leave one to wonder if perhaps I may have been stuck in my grief.

I am aware of and have knowledge of what it means to be stuck in your grief through my observing of other grieving fathers and through my own personal experience. It is a concern that should not be taken lightly, but it is not always continuous. And for anyone who may come across a grieving father like myself, heed this: You can expect to see us mourn for our child forever. And yes, it is also very normal.

> When you pass through the waters, I will
> be with you; and through the rivers, they shall
> not overwhelm you; when you walk through fire
> you shall not be burned, and the flame shall not
> consume you. (Isaiah 43:2 ESV)

Chapter 14

Stuck in Grief

I will give you my offerings to thank you, because you have
saved me from death. You have kept me from being defeated.
So, I will walk with you God in light among the living.
—Psalm 56:11–12 NCV

In the years since my son Nick went to heaven and the progression through my grief began, I have come to believe that God puts others before me to walk alongside me and provide support in this unwanted journey. They have helped me to move forward and carry me if need be whenever I feel that I could no longer go on.

My wife and I have been fortunate in this regard as we have been blessed all these years to be associated with the GriefShare chapter that meets at our church, first as attendees and most recently as facilitators. The thirteen-week Bible-based program provides support for people who are going through the difficult emotions of grief and gives them help in understanding that what they may be going through is normal. Each week, a stand-alone session provides a video with varying topics covered by professional experts in the field of grief, as well as firsthand interviews with others who have traveled the journey of grief themselves. Small discussion groups follow, and the participants hopefully learn and/or share helpful ways of coping with their grief, but most importantly, it is hoped that they will come to understand that they do not have to make the journey alone.

Every grieving parent at some point in their journey comes to realize that their grief, in some form or another, will forever be a part of their lives. And for the grieving father in particular, there is a good chance that they may slip into the secular world's traditional male stereotype of being the strong, protective, and less emotional figure that many expect from them during such a time of crises. But often, by doing so, the result can become the unintentional failure to healthfully work through their own grief, moving unsteadily forward in their journey that often progresses at a snail's pace. Though not exclusive to only fathers in grief, it has been my observation while facilitating at GriefShare and with my father's bereavement groups that dads are the most likely to find themselves at some point in their journey getting stuck in their grief.

One of the last sessions that is covered in the GriefShare program is the topic of "Stuck in Grief." There is an irony though in the timing of this presentation as most attendees are usually still fairly fresh in their grief, and the information shared regarding getting stuck may be too soon to have occurred in those early stages of their grief. But for those of us who may have been on our journey for a while longer, the session does give us the information we need to help us realize that we may be stuck, and it gives us suggestions on how we can cope and ultimately get unstuck.

I admit to having experienced both long-term and short-term periods of being stuck during my grief journey, and since we all grieve differently, it goes to say that we also experience and act to being stuck differently. During my moments of feeling stuck, it has always been the emotional pain that seems to overwhelm me and puts me into those periods of hopelessness. But as the years have progressed, I have come to realize that the pain I am feeling at that particular moment in time does not compare to the pain I experienced at the onset of my grief when it first occurred.

In looking back through my grief journey thus far, I can see that over the years, I have been able to progress to the point of being able to experience the joy of laughing and smiling once again. And perhaps if you too have been stuck or you are stuck now, you are terrified at the thought that the pain you are in will never go way. But let me assure you that the pain you may be feeling now won't always be so constant and present in your every waking moment. But as is the case of the process of grief, I will tell you that unfortunately, some of us will have to go through the pain. But I also want you to know that it doesn't always have to stay in one place, and it doesn't always have to stay stuck.

I opened this chapter with Psalm 56:11–12, and I believe that the most important part of those verses is, "So, I will walk with you God in light among the living." I remember when I first read it, I was feeling stuck, and my initial reaction to it was, "That seems easier to say than it is to do." But over time, as I faced the pain and the fears and accepted the help God has provided for me, I was able to see Psalm 56:11–12 in a different light. I now see it for what God has intended: I should not forget or leave my grief behind but learn to roll with the waves of grief and accept that when the waves are rough, he will take care of me and lead me to the safety of the shore. God wants me to know that though I will always grieve for my son, I can also still live in this world that I am a part of, serve God, and keep my son alive in so many ways by just living.

In the opening paragraph to this chapter, I expressed my belief that God has put others before me to walk alongside me and provide the support I needed to get to the next step in my journey. I have seen that through whomever God has sent before me, his timing has always coincided with a moment in my grief that I truly felt I could no longer go on with my journey. It was as though he knew I was stuck, and by whatever way he chose to intervene for me, I was suddenly infused with the encouragement I needed to continue the journey because that has always been his plan for me to do. And if you have not guessed it by now, it is to God that I give the credit for helping me during those difficult times in my grief to get unstuck, allowing me to move forward on this never-ending journey.

A few years ago, I was asked to lead the session of "Stuck in Grief" during one of our GriefShare meetings. Being a teacher, I wanted to provide some supplemental material to support the information already provided by the GriefShare workbook and videos on the topic of how and when we are stuck, God provides us the means to get out of it and to continue on. In googling to find such material for my presentation, I came upon a short video that I found on YouTube. I strongly encourage you to google "Derek Redmond You Raise Me Up." "You Raise Me Up" is a song that plays along with the video, and I warn you: If you have not seen it before, and even if you have, tears are likely to flow from your eyes.

The video clip is about a man named Derek Redmond. He was a world-class Olympic sprinter from Great Britain who was favored to win a medal at the 1992 Barcelona Olympic Games. But something happened during his race for gold; something happened on the way to his victory.

About a third of the way into the race, Redmond was suddenly immersed in pain as he pulled a hamstring muscle in his leg. So painful was the pull that he dropped onto the track as the other sprinters continued on to the end of the race. Redmond, the competitor that he was, got up and began to literally hop and run on one leg, trying to get to the finish line. But the pain was too much to bear, and he dropped to the ground as the tears and screams from the pain seemed to have put an end to his race. But still, he continued on in his attempt to get up and finish the race, only to fall again.

Just as it seemed that he was going to give up, a man suddenly came running out of the stands toward him, alluding the security guards. He made his way to Derek and promptly helped him to get up, and with his arms supporting him, together they began to painfully move forward toward the finish line. The man was his father, Jim Redmond. He told his son, "We will do this together." As they got closer to the finish line, Jim let go of Derek who then painfully hopped and limped his way across the finish line to the standing ovation and tears of everyone in the stadium.

I think that we can all relate to that tragic event in the life of Derek Redmond. If we were to imagine that the race we were in was about our life and we then took Derek's tragic race and simply put ourselves in his place, it's easy to imagine as our race in life seem to be going well that we too can suddenly experience the pain of falling down in the middle of life's track.

At that moment, we can relate that pain that we are feeling is the death of our sons or daughters. And as we try to get up, we can't help but feel that this isn't happening, that it can't be real. But as we try to get up and we painfully fall down again, it is then that we realize that this is all too real. And yet, as the race continues and we lift our head and look ahead of us, we can still see the finish line, but in truth, it is much more than just the finish line that we are about to mourn.

Whereas Derek Redmond's dream of an Olympic medal was crushed, so too are our dreams now also crushed. But the difference is that it is not the dreams we had for ourselves that we now weep for; in our role as a grieving father, our pain derives from a fact that we don't want to face—the dreams we had for our children that will no longer happen. Graduations, prom dates, weddings, and grandchildren are now all gone, and all we can do is lie down broken on the track of life. This reality makes the pain so bad that we now feel that we can no longer move from where we are now and we no longer care about winning or even reentering the race. But for some reason, we know we have to get to the finish line. But we can't, or we don't know how we can get there. We are stuck.

Like Derek Redmond, as we are stuck in the track and feeling unable to go on, we too are helped by our father who suddenly appears to help us up, letting us lean on him for strength, encouraging us to get back into the race, and pointing the way to the finish line. But in our race, the father I speak of is God. And he is not only there to help us move on, but he is also there to help us move forward from the spot that we are stuck in and to get us to continue moving forward toward the finish line of our race. He lets us know that the victory is not in "winning" the race, but rather, the real victory is about finishing the race.

How can we be benefitted by placing ourselves in a similar position of being stuck in the track like Derek Redmond was? I believe that all of us grieving fathers need to know that God sees us when we are stuck, and he gives us the opportunity to move forward, one step at a time if need be. And he wants us to open our eyes to the world that lies before us. He wants us to know that we need not worry about our child because he has them and we will see them again. But until then, we need to enjoy what God still has for us here. And the best way to honor our child is by continuing to live for and love all those who they left behind for us and for each other, and that includes ourselves.

And by the way, God lets us know that the finish line of our race is heaven and it is there where our reunion with our children will take place. That will be our reward for getting unstuck in our grief and moving forward to finishing the race, just as God has planned for us to do.

> I keep trying to reach the goal and get the prize for which God called me through Christ to the life above. (Philippians 3:14 NCV)

Chapter 15

September

This month is to be for you the first month,
the first month of your year.
—Exodus 12:2 NIV

My mother took me to my first day of kindergarten in the fall of 1965, and until I retired as a high school teacher, every fall from 1965 to 2020, I had a first day of school. I had fifty-six consecutive first days of school to be exact. During the last half of my teaching career, schools began opening earlier at the end of the summer in August. However, for most students and their teachers, at all levels of education, the beginning of the year that most shapes and influences hopes, goals, and growth intellectually, physically, and socially has always surrounded what we call the school-year calendar that traditionally begins in and around Labor Day at the beginning of the month of September.

As fathers, September was a month that we, along with our child, experienced the combination of excitement and fears that came along with the new school year. We watched as our children grew physically and emotionally over their summer breaks and then looked forward to the unknown. Who will their teacher be? Will they have old friends in the same class, or will they make new friends? I often approached it as excited anticipation of the next period in my life.

My son Nick died the winter before he would have entered high school. He was looking forward to that next step in his life, and even though he worried about the bigger and older kids he would walk the campus with, and that included his big brother, JP, he nonetheless looked forward to the new clubs, the activities, dances, elective classes, playing water polo, and probably girls.

It was easy for me to see how my son Nick looked forward to his new school year as I already had the experiences of seeing how my older son, JP, experienced each of his new school years and, even more so, how I approached them as well not just as a former student but also as an educator. I recall every year that I anticipated that my new school year would be the best ever. I looked forward to the fall sports season (I played football), the new classes, and who might be in my class alongside me; and because I chose education as my career, I got to continue to experience it every year throughout most of my adult life as well. So it was that come every September, I got to share a bit of what my sons were also going through on their campus at the same time.

Admittedly, there was an almost magical feeling that would come over me each year as September and the new school year rolled around and the prospect of what was about to come, both as a student and later as a teacher. It was a lifelong feeling I had been going through since I was five years old, and I looked forward to it every single year. But after my son Nick passed away, that all changed. Though I continued to teach and perform my duties involving high school athletics and enjoying them as best as I could, those last ten years of my career before retirement were never the same again. The month of September and the new school year all seemed to have lost its magic.

It seemed very strange that first September after my retirement at not having a first day of school for the first time since I was five years old. There was a sense within me for a week or so that I was supposed to be doing something. Well, if you are either a student or a teacher for fifty-six years, there was bound to be an emptiness at not seeing your colleagues or your students five days a week anymore.

Gone were my 5:30 a.m. arrivals to school to begin my day, along with the stress of getting lesson plans and materials ready, the updating and organizing of the day's athletic events, preparing facilities, and transportation schedules—basically all the logistics necessary to prepare for these contests. But something else was missing. What was missing was the additional stress brought on by my continuing grief for my son that was only compounded by whatever was going on at my place of work, both in good times or bad. Gone was that punch-in-the-gut feeling that could suddenly appear on varying levels as I was no longer being confronted day-to-day with visions of my son every time I faced students in the classroom or anywhere else on campus. And as my first days of school ended, so were the thoughts of the ones Nick missed and would have enjoyed.

I don't know if other fathers who still have other children at home may experience some partial relief from those September feelings I used to have once their last surviving child leaves school and they no longer have to experience their first days of school. But I admit to welcoming it. Now the feelings only return when I make myself recall those days and years, but I can now actually enjoy Septembers again because I no longer have to live with any more first days of school.

In all fairness, not all Septembers in my last ten years as a teacher brought on melancholy moods. One of our greatest joys occurred during September toward the end of my career was when my son JP and daughter-in-law, Kimberly, got married and with their marriage came a precious gift for Kirsti and me in the person of our grandson. It was at this joyous occasion that I also took the opportunity to include my son Nick in his big brother's special day with a physical presence at the wedding.

Early on in our grief journey, my wife had bought me a silver ring that has a small compartment that now contains some of Nick's ashes in it. I made sure to bring it with me and wear it throughout the entire wedding festivities, making sure to pose my finger with the ring on it in as many of the wedding pictures that I could. I had been thinking about doing this even before JP met and had become engaged to my daughter-in-law. It was an obsession of mine to be sure that Nick would have a physical presence at the ceremony. I do not wear that ring all the time, but it is usually part of my everyday accessory that I wear often when I go on vacations or special events.

I have, for example, taken it with me and worn it on our trips to Costa Rica, Europe, Hawaii, and to most of our vacations that I just felt the need to have him with me. It has become a symbolic gesture on my part to remind myself that my son is always with me no matter where I am or when.

And now, September and its first days of school have a different flavor for me that no longer bring on the uneasiness and mixed feelings that I had previously experienced before retirement. Now I enjoy watching as my grandson gets himself all excited for his first days of school, and I look forward to him sharing how his first days went, which of his friends are in his class, what new friends he has now made, and what he thinks of his teacher.

Now I can now look forward to the end of those hot summer days and the beginning of the cooler fall weather that September brings. Now the only time I think about my former first days of school as well as those of JP and Nick's are only when I purposely recall them, and when I do, they tend to be pleasant and happy memories.

Since my retirement, I no longer have to feel the hurt that occurred during the last ten years of my teaching when I saw my students on the campus, sitting before me in my classroom or in an athletic facility, because I can now easily remember how much fun and excitement my son Nick would have at school. And I can now see it in my grandson, who carries the same name as his uncle Nick.

Through him, I can once again appreciate the hopes, goals, and anticipation that he has and that his uncle once did. Together we both look forward to what we genuinely hope will be a good year. I can now thank God for Septembers again and for the reminder of happier first days of schools in my past.

> He will be strong, like a tree planted near
> water that sends its roots by a stream. It is not
> afraid when the days are hot; its leaves are always
> green. It does not worry in a year when no rain
> comes; it always produces fruit. (Jeremiah 17:8
> NCV)

Chapter 16

But What of My Children Still at Home

You have given me many troubles and bad times, but you will give me life again. When I am almost dead, you will keep me alive. You will make me greater than ever, and you will comfort me again.
—Psalm 71:20–21 NCV

The night my son Nick had his accident at home, my wife and I were driven by a neighbor who was a police officer to the hospital as we followed the ambulance transporting our son to the emergency. Needless to say, my son Nick did not make it. My wife lay there in the emergency room, going into shock while being supported by individuals in the hospital, as well as the kids pastor from our church who had rushed to the hospital when he had heard about what happened. I, on the other hand, also in shock and feeling numb, returned to our home with another family friend for the sole purpose to personally inform my oldest son, JP, that his little brother was now in heaven.

I had not yet returned from school when the accident happened, and it was my seventeen-year-old son, JP, who had been there with his mother when it occurred. While my wife and I went to the hospital, he stayed at home with the many friends who had come to our house. Now as Kirsti and I sat staring at the lifeless body that was once our beautiful and jovial son Nick in the emergency room,

I was overcome with the feeling that I needed to rush home and be the one to let our son JP know in person and not by a phone call or by someone else relaying him a message about the terrible news of his brother.

Upon returning to the house, I walked in, and not really seeing or acknowledging those in the room, I made my way to the family room where I found JP and those who were there were waiting with him for me. They all were likely very nervous, awaiting, no doubt, and hoping that there was good news. My eyes immediately fixed on my son JP, and I walked directly toward him. By now, he had risen out of his seat on the sofa and took a few steps to meet me halfway. As we now stood before each other, I thought he knew what I was about to tell him. I was sure that despite what he was about to hear, he was still feeling some glimmer of hope as was reflected in his brave attempt to control any emotional feelings he was subduing otherwise. As we faced each other, it was JP who would calmly ask the question as to the status of his little brother, seeking for the answer that he no doubt hoped would support his glimmer of hope.

In looking back, I think I can remember how he was trying not to rush the question, perhaps it was to delay the inevitable or prepare himself to hold it together. As his father, I could see he was scared. And despite what had happened, my parental instincts set in, and I wanted to shield and protect him from his fear and the bad news I was about to deliver. At that moment, it felt like the room was empty. He and I stood in silence alone, and I, too, was afraid of having to be the one to tell him.

I think we both knew at that moment that the conversation we didn't want to have was about to happen, and as mentioned before, it was JP who spoke first. With as much control as he could muster for a seventeen-year-old who had never experienced this type of tragedy, he asked me the question I wished I didn't have to answer. Holding back in his tone and sensing what I can only describe as fear, he asked me, "Dad, when is Nick coming home?" And in response to JP's emotional question, I replied with the greatest of all pains the words no father should ever have to tell anyone, especially his teenage son: "He's not coming home."

Upon my response, my only concern at that moment was for JP. As we both embraced tightly, I witnessed my son releasing a sudden burst of tears and a cry of anguish that at the time I later thought I fully understood and related to. In the days and weeks that followed, I may have felt that this would be our lifetime shared father-and-son journey of grief and that we would get through this together, or so I thought. But I did not know that the tight embrace of pain and sorrow that we both shared at that moment would unknowingly be the beginning of our separate grief journeys because the loss of a son by a father was always going to be different than the loss of a brother by a sibling as it would be for JP.

It was at that moment that we both embarked on our separate twelve-year grief journeys for Nick. And for all fathers who have lost their sons or daughters, the separate paths taken between them and their surviving children are no different from what I have experienced with my son JP. For though the story of a parent's grief journey and that of a sibling may differ from each other, the paths will always lead to the same destination in the end, heading in the same direction toward the story's conclusion.

As I have shared before, my wife's and my individual grief for our son Nick was different from the one we shared together as his combined mom and dad. This was due to our own unique and individual relationship that we shared with him as a mother and son and as a father and son. Therefore, it goes to say that the unique and individual relationship between JP and his brother would also differ from what Kirsti and I had with Nick.

JP and Nick were four years apart in age, and they loved each other. At the time Nick passed away, their day-to-day relationship was going through some rough patches due to the both of them going through physical and social growing pains, accompanied by the needs and wants that teenagers go through. Despite all that, they still held a shared devotion and loyalty for each other. Together they shared experiences and history with regards to their upraising by Kirsti and me—be they considered good, bad, happy, or sad—but if pressed, they would both admit that it was all mostly good and happy.

I have no doubt that when needed, they sought out each other as a source of comfort from my angry outbursts during the times I believed they may have been misbehaving. Often during those times, they never hesitated to defend each other. I recall shortly before Nick died, I was scolding JP for picking on his brother, and of all the people who jumped to his defense, it was Nick. To be honest, I was actually quite proud of the them for doing so, especially as I usually came around to realizing they were right to do so. (More often than not, my responses to any alleged offense they may have committed were usually an overreaction likely brought on by my work-related issues. Sound familiar, Dads?)

Together as a Contreras brothers' team, they could both reveal a sweet, loving, and kind affection toward both Kirsti and me. Many was the time when they combined their efforts to do nice things for us (more often, rightfully so, for their mother than me). And they both shared a wonderful sense of humor, bringing to our home the gift of their infectious laughter and providing pure joy to our home. And, oh, how they especially loved a good practical joke, most often planned out with the aim of pulling one over on their old man.

Nick and JP also shared a common love of summer and winter adventures, especially water-related activities such as swimming and playing water polo and winter activities such as skiing and snow-boarding. They both loved traveling as a family to Hawaii, they shared a love for *Harry Potter* movies, and they never lost the love of going to Disneyland.

Later, when Nick entered his teen years, they no doubt shared similar tastes in their contemporary music and whatever else teen-agers enjoyed doing that would make their mother and me roll our eyes. I not only loved how they stuck up for each other, even when they were not getting along, but also how devoted they were to their mom, how they loved animals, especially how natural they were around dogs and cats, and of course, how they both were very much alike in how they were fiercely loyal to their friends.

Before Nick passed away, Kirsti and I often shared with each other our personal dreams and hopes for both of the boys. And despite them both being raised in the same house under the same rules, values, and expectations, we were very much aware that they were also two different people. For example, when it came to their common love of adventure, we knew that Nick often approached his need for exhilaration from an activity without regard to self-control, always seeking the immediate fun and gratification that was directly in front of him and rarely looking at the possible results at the end of the adventure ahead. JP could also approach any adventure with as much *gusto* and time unabandon as did his brother, but he also had the ability to understand that at some point ahead on this joyride he may be on, he would eventually see there was a need to prepare to stop before going too far and possibly harming himself or others.

Ironically, when it came to school, Nick could apply some self-discipline once he started an assignment (albeit with some occasional nudge by his mother). He found a certain excitement in envisioning the finished product of his work. He was pretty good at planning it out with his thinking process being, "It's due in a week. I should get started on it now," whereas JP was more of a last-minute type of student, never in a rush to planning it out—if need be, leaving it for later. His thinking process was, "The assignment isn't due till next week. I got time."

Nick loved his friends and being around other people, but he could also find happiness just as easily working and playing on his own. JP, on the other hand, rarely did well playing alone. Even as a child, he was very social, and he always needed to be around other people. They were both smart and intuitive. Nick loved numbers, and he was very artistic, whereas JP was creative when working with technology. And when he applied himself, I always felt that he, like his brother, showed the ability to approach questions and find answers with a scientific mind. Both could be inventive as Nick liked working with his hands and physically building things, whereas JP enjoyed physical bantering. He liked creating things through experimenting as he does often when he is cooking or creating a new recipe, for example.

While Nick was alive, Kirsti and I both understood that we could have separate hopes and dreams for both of them based on where their individual skills, talents, and temperaments lay. But we also understood that we could still hold them to be equally accountable to the same expectations with regard to the values, morals, and consequences that we taught them as they matured year-to-year socially, physically, and intellectually in our home. But after Nick passed away, half of Kirsti's and my dreams for each of our boys ceased to exist. And for a while, the love, hope, prayers, and dreams we once placed for two boys unfairly fell onto the shoulders of the one we still had here on earth—JP.

Before Nick died, we were in the process of preparing JP for the soon-to-be-adult world he would enter upon graduation from high school. While at the same time, we were also preparing Nick to enter high school and begin the process of shaping the foundations he would need once he too found himself in that transitional period of his life as his big brother was then in.

As Kirsti and I were both college graduates, we both assumed that JP and Nick would both go on to college to further their education and use it to establish careers and help with giving them a good foundation once they too married and raised children of their own. But as an educator, I experienced over my entire career that many students who, once they left high school, may not have yet been prepared emotionally or academically to go to college, and I was open to either of my sons—should they need to—taking a different path that I still assumed or hoped may lead to a college education or the equivalent of one at some point in their future.

Though I preferred they both go to college out of high school, I had no qualms about them entering the working world for a time or going to a trade school or even joining the military. I could see the benefits of experiencing the grown-up world, using the real-life education they would receive to decide for themselves what path in life they may want to take—not necessarily the one parents, teachers, and the career-minded world I was professionally a part of tells them they needed to.

Although my wife and I always assumed, hoped for, and even gave some push to both JP and Nick toward a post–high school education in college as the best plan to take, I personally felt that of my two sons, JP was the one who possibly could benefit the most by doing some more growing up after his high school graduation. I could see the value in him experiencing the difficulties of the adult world out there, deciding for himself what his future career choices might be influenced by on what he learned outside of a classroom, and figuring out what he may need from there.

I always felt that Nick would definitely go to college. He was bright and had a variety of skills and interests and could have pursued any number of different paths to take, but still, I just felt that he was destined to go to college. Maybe it was because the skills and interests I thought he excelled at the most were more in tune with what a higher level of education might be able to provide for him to accomplish those goals and interests.

JP, like his little brother, was also blessed with many different talents, skills, and strengths; and he kept an open mind on what it was he would like to pursue in his post–high school goals. But like with so many young adults, many of those interests were not necessarily interrelated, and in hindsight, they reflected what would be his eventual need to experience different paths other than academia. He needed to seek out and experience the adult world in order to distinguish and eliminate those paths that turned out to be passing fancies or that were not practical so that he could eventually prioritize which of his interests would truly fit his personality and talents. But with Nick's passing, I admit to my part in pushing him toward a narrower path that I fear may have limited, at least or a while, in allowing him to grow into where his true interests and talents meshed together and lay.

I have no doubt that many grieving parents are guilty of doing the same thing I did in transferring many of the dreams I had for my late son, Nick, over to my surviving son, JP. In doing so, I also transferred the natural father tendency to worry and the need to protect my remaining earthly child.

When Nick died, I may have, at times, gone overboard—if not in fact than in my mind—by overworrying and being overprotective for my older son, JP. I am sure that, like many other fathers who have lost a child, there comes a fear of the possibility of losing one of their other children. When that occurs, the natural instinct is to protect their surviving children at all costs. After all, as men, many of us fathers were raised on the secular premise that our main job was to protect our family. And as a newly grieving father, we may still be in the mode of feeling guilty, believing we failed to protect our child now residing in heaven.

During those early days of my grief, I can recall driving by his school to make sure his truck was parked and he was safely attending school. I often texted him and grew anxious if he did not answer me in what I thought was a reasonable amount of time, only to finally breathe a sigh of relief when he did eventually reply. I remember feeling guilty after the fact when I once drove by a place that he told me he would be with his friends because I wanted to be sure that he got there safely, but then I worried I may have embarrassed him in front of his friends. And I confess to more than a few times during the night, especially in the first year after Nick passed away, that I found myself unable to sleep. And I would quietly wander and peak into his bedroom, watching carefully to be sure he was breathing in his sleep.

To be honest, to this day, I can still find myself in the role of being the protective father, adding to my worries not just for my now adult son but also for my daughter-in-law and my grandson. Worries, no doubt at times, others may feel are unreasonable, but in my defense, that is what losing a child can do to you.

I will say that when I look back at those moments mentioned above, I have a hard time apologizing for some of my behavior, especially when they occurred, immediately following Nick's death, because at that time I was scared. I was scared because just a short time before, I had two beautiful sons that I was blessed to see every day. One day, I had the luxury of having two separate dreams for each of their futures; and then suddenly, I was faced with having only one son that I could now see every day, touch every day, and physically talk to every day. And of course, there now also existed that underlying fear of any possibility I could lose him too. And even though JP is now an adult with a family of his own, I still can't cease worrying about him because I cannot control those occasions when I am still being scared for him or for me for that matter.

To this very day, no matter where I am, I still make a point of texting him every morning with a Bible verse and a message reminding him to have a good day and that I love him. And even after twelve years since the passing of his brother, I still do not feel at ease until I can feel the welcome relief in my heart that comes whenever I receive his replies.

> Here for the third time I am ready to come to you. And I will not be a burden, for I seek not what is yours but you. For children are not obligated to save up for their parents, but parents for their children. (2 Corinthians 12:14 ESV)

Chapter 17

Siblings Do Not Grieve as We Do

We do not want you to be uninformed, brothers and
sisters, concerning those who are asleep, so that you
will not grieve like the rest, who have no hope.
—1 Thessalonians 4:13 CSB

As I have written before, my personal grief for my son Nick is different than the way my wife Kirsti and I have grieved for him. As combined parents, we both shared a relationship with "our" son, but as individuals, as a mom (Kirsti) and a dad (David), we also had a unique and singular relationship with Nick that was our own and which we didn't necessarily share with each other as husband and wife. That said, as Nick's brother, JP too had his own unique and personal relationship with him, which was not necessarily the same as the ones Kirsti and I had with Nick.

Over the years, as JP, Kirsti, and I have all traveled and progressed through our personal grief journeys, we have also grown in our own relationships with each other. And together we have all moved forward in our shared loss of Nick, our son and brother.

As I have already shared, JP loved his brother, and they were devoted to each other. I have also shared how at the time of Nick's passing, they were going through some rough patches in their relationship. Of course, this is not abnormal for brothers who are going through different stages in their own teenage lives at the same time. But when Nick died, JP, like his mother and I, was in shock; and he experienced emotional pain, which was accompanied by sorrow and tears.

I have always regretted that I was in no position to be of any emotional help to him because I was going through my own shock and my own sorrow, and that kept me from consoling him in the manner that I wanted to and that I believed a father should. But God looked after us by placing family and friends before us during those early days and weeks of our grief. We were so thankful and blessed by those individuals who stepped in and became the emotional support we needed in order to just make it to each day that followed, but eventually, the support given to us by many of these family members and friends came to an end.

As I have said before, through no fault of their own, they eventually moved on with their own lives. By doing so, we were reluctantly left to our new normal, and we were now forced to continue on with our grief as a family among ourselves. And the new normal that we embarked on at that time and continue to live with today was not something that we could avoid. We came to the realization from that point on that our grief was not going to go away, and it would not be the same for each of us.

I have not been shy about sharing my journey—be it through my writings or in my discussions—with grief groups, with my fellow grieving parents, and/or with other grieving fathers. And as I have repeatedly mentioned before, both my wife and I are also very much aware that, over the past twelve years, we have learned to accept that as individuals we have and always will grieve differently for Nick. We are very much aware of this because when we have felt the need to, we have openly shared with each other and/or observed how the other has gone through our own personal grief journeys. But what I have not shared is how our son JP has grieved for his brother over these past twelve years.

Unlike Kirsti and me who have often talked and shared our thoughts about it, JP has not done so, at least with me, in comparison to the same abundance that my wife and I have done so. That is not to say that he does not grieve for his brother; it only says to Kirsti and me what we have already learned and shared about grief during our journey, and that is, of course, that we all do it so differently. And that goes for a sibling grieving for their sibling too.

As for me, JP and I do not have nor have we really ever had long, deep, and emotional conversations with regards to how we are grieving for Nick. Don't get me wrong, we do not avoid it, but it's just that compared to the conversations that I have had with Kirsti or even lesser conversations with, say, my dad or my sister or other fellow grieving fathers, the discussions between JP and me about his brother have often been limited to shorter conversations, the answering of a question about it, or a quick reminder of memories that we may have of Nick. And I have to say that there were times early in my grief journey that this used to bother me, but my reasons for being bothered by it were not fair to JP.

At the time, what I needed was any and all interactions with those who knew Nick and loved him because I needed help to get through my pain. Admittedly, early on, I mistakenly believed that the pain others were going through were the same as mine, and I just could not understand why JP was not sharing with me what I believed to be our shared pain of losing Nick. But over the years, as I have received so much information about grief and more specifically about how to work through grieving for the loss of my son, I have now come to accept that JP is grieving for his brother in his own way. And as I have learned over the years to accept and respect my wife's personal grief for Nick, I have also come to realize that I too must extend that same courtesy to JP. I needed to learn, accept, and respect his personal grief for his brother.

Because my conversations with JP on the subject of grieving for his brother have been fewer than I may have wished or would have at least expected, we have both had to rely often on our own observations of how each other has progressed through our own individual grief process. Over the past twelve years, I have observed that JP does grieve for his brother in his own way and has shown it. For example, initially, he played a major role in the celebration of life with his touching tribute to his brother on the stage at the church, and later, he took the lead in being adamant that we all design and purchase memorial stickers to place on our car rear windows to honor his brother in remembrance.

During the spring of his senior year in high school, he chose not to compete for the varsity swim team, but during the summer after he graduated, he did compete for the swim team that both he and his brother were members of to honor him. And just prior to his graduation, he got his first tattoo on his shoulder that allows him to honor his brother.

The story of that first tattoo also has an additional touching story that has a personal and emotional meaning for him, though he has rarely shared it. The tattoo depicts a young boy (Nick), with unkept hair like his brothers, sitting on a skateboard under a palm tree. (I personally like to think it represents their happy times together in Hawaii.) The boy also has in his hand a sketching pad, meant to represent his brothers love of drawing, which of course was Nick's go-to activity for self-relaxation. Well, there is more to the story of his first tattoo that has a more personal and emotional meaning for JP.

A couple of years into his own grief journey, he had to undergo surgery to repair some damage to his shoulder due to an injury. After the surgery, the doctor who performed the surgery revealed how he had restitched parts of the tattoo because of the incisions. When the doctor asked him about the tattoo, JP proceeded to tell him about his brother, and he made a point of giving the doctor a history of what the tattoo was meant to represent and what it meant to him. Needless to say, the doctor was very touched by what he heard and was happy to have saved the tattoo for him, and in doing so, JP was very appreciative of the doctor preserving the tattoo. The fact that the doctor took the extra time to restore it to as close to its original condition as possible meant a lot to JP, and even though he has since acquired more tattoos, I know that he still holds a lot of pride for that first one and what it has come to mean to him. It is how he has chosen to keep a part of his brother with him forever.

There was a second story that till now was unknown to me until I asked JP to proofread this part of the book for accuracy, errors, or missing information because of the part he played in it. I'll let his own words from a text he sent me tell the story after he finished reading it.

> Just calling to say I read that packet you gave me. I like it. I have no quants or qualms over it. I did notice during the tattoo part. Maybe I failed to mention or perhaps it was forgotten with the passage of time, but my shoulder tattoo wasn't just stuff Nick enjoyed. He drew all that himself. That whole shoulder tattoo (sans the name "Nick") was all original art done by him. Robin's dad (the artist) took all his art and spent like a week drawing his art over and over making it, so Nick's skateboard, art supplies, and even his character were drawn by Nick.

After reading JP's message to me, I immediately left him a message thanking him for sharing what I had not known before. I then shared it with my wife, guessing that he didn't tell us back when he got it because at the time, he knew we were never big fans of tattoos. But more likely, during that time in our shared grief, he often tried to limit this type of information to his mother and me in an almost protective way because he did not want to see us be further hurt or going through any more emotional pain than we already were in. Ironically, just prior to my giving him the packet to read, my wife and I had been discussing how JP had always kept much of his grief for his brother to himself, so the timing could not have been more appropriate for me to see and to share with my wife. (I later learned she was already aware of it, but she had always assumed JP had told me as well.)

I could not say enough how thankful we were that JP let us know how he chose to have his first tattoo be so personal. The fact that JP recognized his brother's artistic gifts while he was here and that he wanted to honor him permanently for having them meant the world to his mother and me. But I have to say that what really stands out for me is the fact that he purposely meant to have his brother be with him literally forever, which in my opinion speaks volumes to his unspoken love and respect for Nick and our shared family values.

As the years have moved forward in our mutual grief, JP has, in his own way, continued to progress in his journey, whether it be in sharing with us balloon releases marking his brother's angelversary and, when the time was right, introducing his brother in spirit to his son as his "uncle Nick," and by not discouraging him from calling or introducing himself as "Nick Contreras" to members outside the family.

JP even surprised many of us at the wedding of one of his best friends in which he served as the best man, when during his speech at the reception, he thanked him for being supportive of him by including in his speech how much he appreciated his support, and I quote, "...after I lost my brother." But JP saved his greatest remembrance of his brother when in a private moment with his mother prior to his own wedding, he told Kirsti, "If Nick were here, he would be my best man." And even though he said that to Kirsti and not me, when she shared that conversation with me, it made my heart burst with so much pride for him. It allowed me the thought that Nick was there in spirit and in the hearts of all of us who loved him and who he loved on that very special day for JP, Kim, and our family.

I do wish at times that JP would let me into his heart so that we could share remembrances of Nick and our shared love for him more often, but he has chosen in his own way to keep grief more personal and to walk through his grief journey for his bother in the manner he feels most comfortable within his own heart.

Many other fathers who may read this book may likely have their own surviving children whose grief will vary from parent to child and siblings to siblings. Some fathers may find it easy to share with them, and some may have their surviving sons or daughters be even less open about it than JP is with me. If they have multiple surviving children, they will likely find that each one of them will have had a personal relationship with their sibling in heaven, and that may bring to light their different grief journeys among themselves. But it is important not to mistake their surviving children's personal grief as seemingly less than or more than ours or less unique than others who are also grieving.

As we recognize that we may grieve differently from each other as mothers and fathers, we also need to remember that siblings do not grieve as we do, but they do grieve; and as a family, we need to be there and be supportive of each other if and when it is needed during the grieving process.

> There is a time for everything.... A time to be born and a time to die, ... A time to embrace, and a time to say goodbye. (Ecclesiastes 3:1,2,5b NIV)

Chapter 18

October

Now I commend you because you remember me in everything
and maintain the traditions even as I delivered them to you.
—1 Corinthians 11:2 NIV

The days of October have often had an anticipatory effect on
me. October, in my eyes, represents the soon-to-be conclusion of
a year soon to end and the eventual introduction to what will be
another new year to come. And it has become a bit of a tradition in
my family that October marks the kickoff for the holiday season,
commencing with Halloween—followed in a timely fashion with the
worldly recognized holidays of Thanksgiving, Christmas, and New
Year's—and will conclude with a major family event better known as
my wife's, Kirsti's, birthday.

Of course, now that the holiday season, commencing in October
and concluding after my wife's birthday, also marks the sad memory
of my son Nicks passing; the recollection of that initial shock of pain
has marked the beginnings of my lifelong journey of grief for my
son. But as the years have progressed forward, they also remind me
of how my son Nick absolutely loved this time of year as well as any
and all reasons to celebrate throughout the entire year, leaving with
me a gifted memorial of mementos, both physically and mentally,
that remind me of all that he loved about life and the celebrations
that come with it.

When we lose loved ones, there are always memories left behind to remind us of their very real presence that once filled a huge part of our lives but now provide us with what at first may feel like sad memories of what once was. With time, these memories will eventually give way to thoughts of happiness, generating smiles for what they gave to us while they were here and now leave behind for us to be treasured memories. But for those of us who are grieving parents, the gradual progression from our initial sadness does give way to an eventual acceptance that what is left behind in the form of physical mementos can be cemented in our hearts as happy memories. It would be wrong to think of mementos and memories as the end or the final destination of grief while we are here on earth. Grieving for a child is never-ending, and those treasured memories are always left open-ended, allowing for triggers that will be a constant reminder of what once was. They will also bring us back often to what could have been and what should have been and sometimes painfully remind us just as often of what and who is missing.

When my mother passed away over twenty-three years ago, the initial sadness of her leaving us eventually evolved into the happy memories that now reside within our minds and in our hearts of the times we had with her while she was still alive and with us. Once more, my mother died knowing that she left my brother, sister, and me with the knowledge that we knew that she gave to us a lifetime of unconditional love, life's lessons, her personal sacrifices, and the examples and tools that, should we choose to use them, will allow us to continue living on and giving to her grandchildren what she gave to us. In other words, she went to heaven satisfied, knowing she had done her parental duties well.

I know as a surviving son that I am not alone in having lost a parent like my mother, who was able to provide for me the unconditional love only a parent can. Because of our earthy relationship, I have no sad memories of her passing away because I am very much aware of the legacy she left for me as a result of our shared time together. I cannot speak for my brother and sister, but for me, there was a final destination and conclusion here on earth for the emotional relationship that I had shared with my mother. The truth is that I do not apologize for not feeling long-term sadness about the end of my relationship with my mother after she died. We had no loose ends or regrets between us because of the abundance of love and happy memories she left me that I will treasure till my own dying days. That is what she willed to me as an emotional inheritance. But alas, as a father, I cannot say the same with regard to the loss of my son Nick.

That the initial sadness of losing my son has eventually progressed toward an overwhelming amount of happy memories for when he was here with me, it does not mean it is equal to the memories left by my mother after she died. Unlike with my mother's passing and her symbolically leaving to me an inheritance for all that she did for me, I was not fortunate to be able to do the same for Nick. In the case of losing my son, there will always be an open-ended wound caused by what many of us know to be an unnatural cycle that comes with the losing of your child. What my mother left to me as her legacy and that is something I too will be able to leave to my older son, JP, is sadly something I cannot leave as a similar legacy to my son Nick because he has gone to heaven before me.

It is not my intention for this chapter to predominantly focus on how the emotional roller coaster of losing your child can affect the memories you carry of his or her life. But I do want to share how my son Nick has left to me a treasure chest full of happy memories and how they have left me with a determination to never forget him and to make sure that I will never let others forget him either. I have also taken comfort in giving myself some relief from any guilt on my part as a surviving dad that I may feel for not having gone to heaven before him and denying myself the natural cycle of life in not being able to leave him a piece of me. Instead of leaving to him a legacy like my mother left to me, I find instead that I can take great pride in how it is he who has left me a legacy of himself to embrace, to be grateful for, and to keep him alive in my heart until I get to see him again.

In my previous book, *Forever 13*, I shared a story about a father who had lost his two-year-old son over sixty years ago. So deep was the pain that he refused to have pictures of him around the house or to have anyone bring up his name in his presence while he was alive.

After he passed away, his eldest surviving son was going through his wallet when he came upon a worn-out photo of that very same two-year-old little boy. Apparently, he had carried it around with him in his wallet for his entire life. That story was shared with me a few years before my son Nick passed away, and I really couldn't tell you if it had any influence on me doing something similar with regard to Nick. But I have, for all these years since Nick passed away, carried a wallet-size photo of him in my wallet. I have one of those wallets that opens up to a two-sided window flap that on each side you can carry what is usually your license and perhaps a photo of your spouse on the other side. But when I open up my wallet, it is not my driver's license that will be staring at me, but instead, the first thing I see every time I open my wallet is a picture of my son Nick when he was about seven years old.

I know I am not the only father who may carry around a picture of his late son or daughter in their wallet as a personal way to honor him; as a matter of fact, I know and/or have heard of others who have found their own unique way to honor their child and, by doing so, carry them on their person throughout their journey. For example, I know of one grieving father who, like my son JP did, got a tattoo with his daughter's name so that he could carry her around on him forever.

Another grieving father I know has kept the last recording of a phone message his son sent him, and though he doesn't listen to it as often as he used to, he still finds comfort in just knowing he has it with him. He finds comfort in knowing that it is available to him twenty-four hours a day and seven days a week for those times he feels the need to hear his son's voice. In addition, he finds that it eases his mind to know that by doing so, he will never forget the sound of his voice.

The mementos made known to me that were chosen by other grieving dad's and mothers are many, and they vary from wearing their son's favorite hoodie (that would be my wife) to a dad wearing his daughter's high school class ring around his neck on a chain or a mother wearing one of her daughter's favorite pieces of jewelry. I have yet to know of any that I find odd or that I would even disapprove of because I understand that as we grieve in our own ways, we also need to realize the manner by which each grieving parent chooses to keep their child close to their heart should be respected as well.

As for me, though I have many mementos of Nick that I hold dear, and when asked, I don't mind sharing, there are four that seem to consistently have a permanent place in my heart as I go through each year of taking my son's memory along with me. They are in no particular order: a guitar pick, a cell phone screenshot, a special ring that I have worn on the ring finger of my right hand, and as I have already shared, a photo I carry permanently in my wallet.

Having already shared the photo I keep in my wallet, I need to confess that the one presently in my wallet is actually the third photo I have used all these years. The first one I accidentally destroyed when I submerged my wallet in water after I jumped in the pool having forgotten to remove it from the pocket in my swim trunks. At the time, I was very upset about what happened to the picture, but I later realized that Nick would have gotten a kick out of it and would have probably laughed at his dad for having made such a dumb mistake. A second photo that I used later was from one of my favorite pictures of him, but after a couple of years, it got torn and worn out, becoming so fragile that I chose to replace it with a third photo. The photo I now presently use is one of him in fourth grade, and he is wearing a blue shirt, which I like seeing him in because blue is my favorite color. Every once in a while, someone will see it when I take out my wallet and comment what a good-looking boy he is, and I smile, thank them, and say, "I couldn't agree more."

The second memento that means a lot to me is a guitar pick that he used when he played his guitars. He had three guitars—two electric guitars that he made in his woodshop at school and a third one that was an acoustic guitar that my sister, Linda, and my brother-in-law, Mark, bought him for Christmas. It was with that guitar that he tried in vain to teach me how to play, using that very pick. Of course, I was a terrible guitar student, and no matter how hard he tried, he was unable to help me with my clumsy fingers. Eventually, he gave up and told me to stick to playing the radio. After he passed away, I found his pick in his room, and I put it into my wallet where it stayed until the day I soaked my wallet. At that point, I decided to safely place it elsewhere because I was afraid of losing it if I ever lost my wallet because after all, I can always get another wallet and another photo. But if I lost that pick, let's just say that losing it in my eyes would be irreplaceable.

The third memento that I keep with me on a constant basis is the picture on my cell phone that is my semipermanent screenshot. It is semipermanent because, depending of the occasion, I have been known to temporarily replace it with other family photos on a strictly temporary basis, but after a short time, I always return to the one I have now. It is originally from a picture we used at his celebration of life, but it was later enhanced to include a Christmas-themed border around his portrait. This was done when my wife submitted it to be used for an ornament at one of the Christmas candle-lighting ceremonies that we attend every year. The ornament that the organizers of the event made is then placed on a Christmas tree display during the ceremony.

I truly cherish this screenshot as it is with me all the time, and it allows me to see him every day and every time that I use my cell phone. This, along with the photo in my wallet, is one of the two most permanent mementos that I have with me all the time, and they help me to remember that he is still with me in my heart. In my own way, they make me feel as though he is always physically with me. The last of the four mementos that I hold a special place in my heart is one that I initially used to have with me as often as my wallet and cell phone, but I now only bring it out on special occasions.

Early on in the first year of our grief, my wife, Kirsti, purchased some mementos that incorporated some of Nick's ashes for us to either wear or put on display. In my case, we purchased a silver ring imbedded with his birthstone, and within the ring was a small compartment from which we could, and later I did, place some of his ashes. I wore it religiously on my right ring finger as a reminder that my son was just not with me emotionally, but in a sense, he was also with me physically as well. It was my permanent way of looking at my finger, touching it, feeling it, and allowing me to feel his presence.

I made a point of taking Nick with me everywhere via the ring. I took it on vacations, work-related conference trips, and important family events or trips. I took the ring to our trip to Costa Rica, a trip that was supposed to be his and Kirsti's, and I took it with us when we finally returned to vacationing in Hawaii. I wore it as part of my everyday jewelry to school and to church on Sundays, and I wore it to our Christmas mornings at his memorial bench at church. So often was it on my fingers that I often forgot I had it on while doing physical labor around the house or wearing it during physical exercises and activities such as hiking, kayaking, swimming, and lifting weights at the gym. I literally wore it out until one day, while doing some gardening, the bottom part of the ring that encircled my finger cracked and broke. Luckily, all of the pieces were not lost, and I actually tried to continue wearing it by rolling athletic tape at the bottom of it. Eventually, I began to fear it would fall off and get lost for good, so I stopped wearing it for a while, intending to fix it at some point in the future. Well, that future moment would come in the form of a special family event that was to be his brother's, JP's, wedding.

As far as a few years into my grief, it wasn't rare for me to have moments of sorrow or pain as I imagined what big family events that Nick would not be present at that he would have otherwise been a part of, but due to his passing, he would no longer be there. One of the major prospective events that I always got uneasy feelings about whenever it crossed my mind was how I would feel on the day that his brother, JP, would be getting married. I had always imagined that, like at my own wedding when my brother, Robert, stood as my best man and I did so at his wedding as well, the day would come when they too would both be the best man for each other at their own weddings. When the day came that my son JP had set his own wedding date, I set myself the goal of being bound and determined that Nick would be there too—not just in spirit but in my mind, physically as well.

Because JP's wedding was to be out of state, I had made plans for the ring with Nick's ashes to be my way of having him at his brother's wedding. As the days got closer and closer to Kirsti and me embarking on our flight to the destination of the wedding, I found myself looking for a jeweler who could solder the ring to make it whole again. It was my plan to wear the ring at the wedding, thus fulfilling my self-promise of having Nick be a part of his brother's wedding. Unfortunately, my luck at being able to find such as a service was not going well.

To no real fault of any of the establishments I was approaching, the timing, cost, and personnel who could do the task for me were just not available. And to say the least, I was getting very nervous as time was running out. Eventually, I did find a shop that did exclusive repairs of intricate novelty goods, which include fine jewelry. By now, it was coming down to a few days before we would leave, and the pricing and timing were leading me to realize that my plans were possibly in doubt. But it is at these moments when you just feel that you just have to trust that God has a hand on whether these types of things are going to be carried out or not.

Once I found a place that could do the job and after I gave them a quick history of my dilemma by explaining to them what I needed to be done and the reasons why, I then held my breath for the answer I was anticipating and not looking forward to hearing. I truly expected the worst after I told them my timetable and how soon I would need it done in order to take it with me on our flight. I truly believed that the answer would be, "Sorry, there just isn't enough time." Fortunately, as luck would have it, the individual that I spoke to as I recall had a glimmering of empathy in his eyes as he told me he would do it and that he would have it done in time for me to take it with me to JP's wedding. Not only did they come through as promised, but they charged me well below what they normally would have for such a service. I don't know if I will ever need to use their services again, but I am forever grateful that I was directed to them and for the service they did for me. I really can't say if my expression of gratitude and thanks toward them was enough or was truly understood, but the role they were playing in my being able to carry out my goal of Nick having a physical presence at the wedding of his big brother was huge. I truly hope somehow that God has let them know.

The only one whom I had shared what my purpose for having the ring on my finger at the wedding with was my wife, Kirsti.

Throughout the ceremony, I admit to making a point of having my hand with the ring on appear in as many wedding photos that I could manage. But while doing so, it never escaped me that this day was my son JP's and my daughter-in-law's, Kim's, big day. Other than my purposeful actions of having the ring in a lot of the pictures, I did not want in any way to take anything from why we were there, which was the celebration of my son and daughter-in-law's marriage. And because only Kirsti had any knowledge of what I was doing below the scenes, I did my best to be sure I made the event to be all about JP and Kim's day.

Now that the ring has been repaired, I have made it a point to bring it out more often for special occasions and for the express purposes of wanting my son Nick's presence to be with me so that I can share if only in my own mind. Not wanting the ring to return to the fragile state that forced me to find a way to have it repaired, I now limit when I do bring it out, but when those days occur, I so enjoy knowing that he is with me. What follows is a sample list of when Nick, via the ring, has been included in what I deem to be special occasions:

- I wore the ring when we attended my father's ninetieth birthday celebration down in Southern California because I wanted Nick's presence, even if only known to me, to be there along with his brother and his cousins. In other words, I wanted all my dad's grandchildren to be there on his special day. That evening, I even made a reference to Nick when speaking at the ceremony on how my dad did not fear death because he had accomplished all he wanted in this life and that he knew that waiting for him in heaven would be not just be my mother and his parents but also his grandson Nick.
- I also took the ring with me on the first combined vacation to the Big Island of Hawaii with JP, Kim, and Nicholai, giving to me the feeling of having my entire family together in our special place.

- I also took it when we all made a long weekend trip to see Yosemite in all its winter beauty. Yosemite is a place we had always intended to take both the boys, but as a result of his passing, we were never able to take Nick, so I took the ring with me when we did go with JP, Kim, and our grandson, Nicholai.
- I continue to bring it with me when we go on our annual angelversary weekend with my sister, Linda, and brother-in-law, Mark.
- I continue to wear it on my finger at my church when sitting on his memorial bench as I bring in the Christmas morning sunrise at what has become Nick and my annual Christmas tradition every year on December 25.

As I mentioned earlier in this chapter, because I respect every grieving parent and how their unique relationship with their child and how they grieve them is their own, I would never question or judge why, how, or what any grieving parent may choose to carry with them as a personal memento in order to remember their son or daughter. With regards to my own choices that I have shared, I am not ashamed that I do have these mementos, and I do cherish them, and I will continue to do so in order to keep my son alive inside of me in any way that I can. Because I know there are so many other fathers or mothers who do the same, it comforts me to know that I am not alone. How I choose to remember my son won't stop for me just as it won't stop for those who are also walking a similar journey as mine.

> When someone you love becomes a memory, the memory becomes a treasure. (Author Unknown)
>
> Some say you are too painful to remember, I say you are too precious to forget. (Author Unknown)

Chapter 19

November
Carrying on Whose Work?

Do people really gain anything from their work? I saw the hard work God has given people to do. God has given them the desire to know the future. He does everything just right on time, but people can never completely understand what he is doing.
—Ecclesiastes 3:9–10 NCV

I retired as a high school history teacher and athletic director two years ago, and almost immediately, I became the recipient of a lot of advice from well-meaning people on how to begin this new chapter of my life. Examples of their ideas for me included "You need to get a hobby"; "Get yourself on a regular schedule, have a routine"; "Volunteer at churches and senior citizens centers"; and "You would be a natural to volunteer at the schools!" And as much as I appreciated their advice, except possibly the one about volunteering at the schools, I preferred to take the first year to symbolically sit back, rest, and do nothing.

After a combined fifty-six years of going to school every day, beginning as a five-year-old in kindergarten, both as a student and later for thirty-six years as a high school teacher with only taking breaks for my unpaid summers, I was more than happy to just take a deep breath and exhale. Frankly, as far as full-time work, I had never known anything else, and admittedly, I never thought of doing anything else other than going to school. And if I am to believe the words of other people who knew of my work as an educator as truthful, I can surmise to myself that I did my job well. Those kind words mean a lot to me because I have always felt that being an educator was the one thing that I truly felt I was both skilled and successful at, but after thirty-six years in the education profession, I truly felt that I needed that first year after retirement to just wind down.

Once I went through my year-long self-debriefing over my long career, only then did I consider my options and interests and search my heart to find a purpose to occupy my post-teaching career. Encouraged by my wife, Kirsti, and friends who had seen samples of my writing skills, I decided to try writing. Initially, my purpose to begin writing was and still is for my own mental and emotional well-being; but to my surprise, I also found that in doing so, I may have also been offering help to other grieving parents as well by letting them know that they are not alone.

For all of us who are grieving throughout the year, the working world is sort of a reminder that within our new normal, our old normal still lingers, and that the working world we are part of in our everyday culture does not necessarily adapt to or fully understand what we are going through. This is a sad reflection in our culture because the perception of the working world of America is that it has a seemingly unempathetic view and that after the grieving worker has been given a few contractual days off to grieve, it is expected that everything will then be back to business as usual. Though this attitude and/or business practice is not indicative with all American employers, its occurrences are enough to give many of them the reputation, earned or not, of seemingly being heartless to the emotional needs of an employee in grief because of the bottom line. And I believe to the grieving father, it heaps a heavy emotional burden on us as we return to work.

I was fortunate in my particular work environment to have been given a more empathetic experience from my school after having lost my son Nick. For one, my boss had also experienced losing his stepson, so even during times that our working relationship was going through either good or not so good times, when it came to empathy for my loss, he was very supportive. Then, of course, there was the familiarity of and the knowledge of all the individuals concerned with my tragedy. Before both my boys began attending their own schools in the community we lived in, they often came to my school with me during summer breaks and/or other events on campus, and many of the staff knew them and were—therefore, for the most part—very supportive. Because of all the above, I was blessed to be the recipient of such kind treatment once I returned to work.

But even though my school often took on the atmosphere of being a temporary safe place for me to grieve outside my home, there were still two for lack of a better phrase, "friendly camps," among my colleagues when it came to the manner in which they showed and gave me support. There were, of course, those who due to fear or ignorance could not begin to fathom what I may be going through and/or what they could say or do. This caused some of them at times to inevitably turn and walk the other way to avoid me in the event we both found ourselves approaching each other in the hallways. By doing this, it freed them from asking me how I was doing or to avoid feeling uncomfortable if I should bring up my son during a conversation, which I likely would have. But I have never held a grudge against those who seemed uncomfortable in my presence; after all, I may have not been much different at dealing with someone I knew who lost a child before I had lost my son. But I am grateful for those who were not hesitant to show their sincere concern for my welfare and who gave me the support I needed and appreciated when I did return to work.

Early on in my grief, there were thankfully a number of colleagues who didn't try to avoid me and who never hesitated to recognize my loss and would say my son Nick's name. They could sense that even if it seemed to hurt, and initially it did, I truly appreciate whenever they would bring up a story to share about him. I also treasured how they would politely listen to me with genuine kindness and empathy whenever I told stories of Nick myself because they may have sensed in me my need to remind everyone how special he was. I was also very touched by how they would ask how my wife, my older son, JP, and I were doing at home as we had begun to navigate our way through each day as we grieved for our Nick. And even though I rarely took them up on it, I so appreciated how they never hesitated to remind me that if I needed anything, all I had to do was ask. But alas, often, depending on the situation, this group of colleagues was usually in the minority among the total staff on campus; and the early attention to my situation numbered less and less as the days, weeks, months and years progressed further and further away from the time of Nick's passing.

In defense of all my work colleagues and through no fault of their own, it was the passing of time that resulted in the natural process of them moving on with their own lives and careers. It was not that any of them didn't care about me any longer, but for many of them, they still had to continue to deal with the day-to-day issues of our profession. Besides the concerns my colleagues had for my grieving, they also had to deal with the everyday concerns for their working conditions, their professional goals, and the constant stress that goes with being public high school educators—not to mention dealing with their own personal lives and their own families outside of school life.

I myself was also forced to move forward professionally alongside of them for many of those same reasons, but as a grieving father, I continued to carry with me the additional day-to-day emotions of grief for my son Nick.

What many would have rarely seen or notice about me during this time was that as I continued my day-to-day and year-to-year work as an educator, there was always a spiritual-like presence of my son accompanying me that I tried to keep hidden underneath my outwardly appearance on campus. As I taught my classes—intermingled with the students, staff, and parents—they may have never realized that for the last ten years of my career, Nick was always with me, never leaving my side and constantly in my heart and in my thoughts. For the remainder of my career following my son's passing, my responsibilities to my students, my colleagues, and my school would always be influenced in some form or another by the progress of my grief for Nick, as well as later with the progress of my wife's, Kirsti's, battles with cancer.

Nick passed away in January of 2011, and I retired over ten years later in June of 2021. When I think about those last ten years of my professional career, it seems that time took a long time to go by. However, when I think about my grief journey and my memories of Nick, time has travelled at a different pace in my mind. When I think back at my time at work, ten years ago felt like ten years ago. But when it comes to thinking about of my son's life, including when he went to heaven, the last twelve, soon-to-be thirteen, years when he was last with me here on earth always feel slow-moving, as though it was just yesterday that I physically saw him last. I believe that this take on how time travels fall in line with the way I approached work after Nick passed away and how I went about my days, weeks, and even years.

When I have brought up the "new normal" in my everyday life in this book, it should be noted that this applies to all areas of my life, including work. For every grieving father, how much their new normal affects their working lives can be different when compared to how it affects another grieving father. This should not be a surprise to anyone because I think we can all agree that we all grieve differently and how it affects our work could depend on the work itself. By the work, I am referring to the type of work, the industry the work falls under, the people you work with, and the overall progress of your grief journey while you work.

When I retired, I was a high school history teacher, and a sometimes physical education teacher. By the time of Nick's passing away, I was no longer coaching, but I was by then the school's long-time athletic director. Because I had an administrative credential, I was also, at times, pulled out of the classroom on any given day to be the acting administrator in the absence of my school administration, and I also helped with school discipline and supervision when needed. In addition to my jobs on campus, I served as an executive committee member with the California Interscholastic Federation, (CIF), which is the governing body for high school sports in the state of California, and I later finished my career as the president of the teachers union in my school district. So upon returning to work, my plate was already full, and I found myself not just preparing to clear my plate but doing so while also working with my grief.

The duties and responsibilities at my work described above were the ones that I had been responsible for before my son Nick passed away, and except for a few years when I walked away from day-to-day high school athletics on our campus, they would pretty much be the same duties and responsibilities when I returned to overseeing the athletic department prior to my retirement. However, there was one difference: I was not the same man who had previously held those positions.

When I returned to work after my son died, my new normal brought on by my son's passing had effectively reshaped me emotionally. As a part of the collateral effects my new normal had on me, I now looked at the world through different eyes, and what I was going through emotionally and physically in my personal life would also influence how I approached my job. Bottom line is that the loss of my son had changed me forever from the man I was before, and that change transferred over to the man I was at work as well.

As I brought my new normal with me when I returned to work, I began to look differently at the objectives and priorities of the educational and athletic goals of the school, and more importantly, I began to be more aware of the needs of the people I worked with and whom I supervised and who I served. I became more empathetic and understanding of the struggles of my fellow staff members, my students and student-athletes, and my coaches, as well the concerns of supportive and/or difficult parents. I found myself taking more time to listen and consider different sides of an issue and not being so quick to judgement.

When it came to how others now saw how I had changed, I could sense in those who were aware of what had transpired in my life, becoming more accepting of those differences in me. I saw this by the ways in which they approached me, both personally and professionally, how they spoke with me, and how they accepted those times when I made decisions differently than I normally would have done previously before Nick's passing. But one thing I can tell you is that in the industry of education or in the working world in general, the responsibilities and expectations of the job itself within the industry it occupies do not change. And that seems so regardless of the personal changes to one who may be grieving and whose new normal has changed them forever may be accepted. A grieving father who returns to work after the loss of their child more often than not may get sincere empathy from coworkers, bosses, and customers, on a personal level—or in my case, from parents and students as well. But once he returns, he is expected to pick up his duties that went along with those jobs as before. Therefore, the grieving father needs to be prepared to understand that in the working world, the attitude is that grief is personal, and it should remain so. And it should not affect the job and/or the services expected to be provided.

Though I hold no ill will toward any parents or students at my school who may have given little regard to my situation when wanting their needs addressed, in their defense, many were not made aware of my loss. I did see that once I returned to work, it would be up to me to find that common ground to work through with my grief and perform my duties effectively once I resumed them at school. And as I look back on what transpired during my last ten years at my school—such as my applying and interviewing for new positions at other schools for positions I was ultimately not chosen for—I can see that God had his plans for me to remain where I was. I can see that staying put was not just for my own personal good, but it was also for the good of others who would need me as much as I needed them. God made use of what I had been going through, and what I was continuing to go through, in order that along with others through our combined strength, could press on to the next day.

When we return to work after the death of our child, all the headaches and tumultuous politics of the job return to us, having never really disappeared, and we are forced to jump back into grappling with them in addition to the added burden of our accompanying grief. But some may find some solace in returning to work, if only to temporarily relieve themselves from the constant reminders at home of their loss and the emotional pain that comes with it. It should be noted, however, that you don't "forget about it" completely or even temporarily; you just simply give yourself some relief time from having it being the only thing that occupies your every waking moment and thoughts.

In my case, returning to the responsibilities of teaching my students, working with coaches and student-athletes, dealing with parents, and having to return to supervising, scheduling, and over-seeing athletic contests—all gave me something else to think about, allowing me to expend some of my energy while continuing to work through my grief. And in most cases, these "temporary distractions" allowed for me during the working day to give some emotional time to other issues so that I could, when the time arrived at the end of my work day to return home and to think more clearly when I resumed the work necessary to continue to move forward progression in my grief journey.

One positive thing about returning to work as I have shared before is that while you are there, you are likely to receive some much-needed support from those colleagues whom you have spent so much of your waking hours with over the years while working. Though some may rarely if ever see you in your more personal and intimate moments away from work, it is likely those closest to you at work may be some of the first to notice the changes in you brought on by your new normal. And those whose response and acceptance of you, the grieving man whom they work with, are actually very instrumental in helping you to transition from the old you with the new you in the work environment you all share.

> So I realize that the best thing for them is
> to be happy and enjoy themselves as long as they
> live. God wants all people to eat and drink and be
> happy in their work, which are gifts from God.
> (Ecclesiastes 3:12–13 NCV)

Prior to losing our children when they went to heaven, we could distinguish between friends and work friends, and those relationships may or may not have been inclusive or exclusive to being at work and/or at home. Either way, the relationships that you share with many of your colleagues at work may vary, but there is likely some who are close enough to you that you can open up in a manner that perhaps you don't feel you can share with some members of your family. Not to say you won't put on a brave face at work among your colleagues, but to some specific close friends at work, you don't have to put on that aura that you do at home because you don't feel pressure around them or a responsibility to be the strong and protective member of the family.

Also, what I have learned throughout my time as a GriefShare facilitator is that often you may find others whom you did not expect to be supportive for you, who step up and become a rock you can lean on, holding you up by providing words of encouragement and walking alongside of you when you never expected them to. Of course, it is at these times you may also find out that there are those who unknowingly to you may unfortunately share the same type of loss that you have just experienced. When that happens, whether you are already social friends or not, there is a bond created between you that at any time, when the need arrives, you can be with and understand what each other may be going through. Be it at work, church, or the neighborhood, child loss automatically and reluctantly makes you members of an exclusive club that none of you wished to be fellow members of; but we, nonetheless, appreciate that we are there for each other, and we all recognize that none of us have to be alone in our loss.

In the ten years that passed between my losing Nick and my eventual retirement, I had settled into my new normal and found that common ground I needed to do my job and carry on with my grief. During that time I found I not only embraced those who gave me support, but in turn I found that it was God's plan that I would finish my career where I worked because he could foresee that I would be needed to give support to others like myself who were in the that unwanted position of being grieving parents like me.

I had a former colleague named Dan who retired from the same high school I taught at a couple of years after I began working there who I remembered as a very good teacher and football coach and who I respected as a good Christian man as well. But unfortunately, he earned even greater respect from me after we reconnected a couple of years into his retirement. My admiration for my former colleague grew sadly as I witnessed the manner by which he carried himself throughout his own grief journey after he lost his adult daughter. Unknowingly to the both of us, he was helping to set a foundation for me as I was about to embark on a similar journey as his.

It was a few years after Dan lost his daughter when he reentered my life while attending my son Nick's celebration of life. He approached me and made a point of telling me if I needed to talk, he would be there for me. Ironically, when I began attending the father's bereavement group, he also showed up and began attending too. I believe God placed him in my life to eventually become a supportive, fellow grieving father. We remained close in that relationship both as fellow Christians and as grieving fathers until he passed away from cancer years later. If I am to be honest though, his passing away did not generate tears from me because I recognized there was a silver lining in the path God had set for him. One of the first thoughts I had when I was told of his passing away was not that of sorrow because you see, to all of us who knew him, we were feeling joy, not just for his now being in the presence of God in heaven but also for his much-anticipated reunion with his daughter.

Because of the example he showed to me in his grief journey, I would later find myself in similar positions of using my own experience to be of support for other grieving parents. During the last years of my career, while I concurrently progressed in my own grief journey, I found myself unexpectedly being in a position to support four of my colleagues who would unfortunately lose their children while I was still teaching at my school.

One colleague, who was my executive assistant while I was the athletic director and a part-time assistant principal, lost her son to cancer. Her son happened to have been both my former student and student-athlete, and I was honored to coach him on the varsity baseball team. She had always been one of my most supportive friends after I lost my son, and later, because she was aware of my wife's battles with cancer, she often reached out to me when her son was diagnosed with cancer and went through treatments. When he passed away, I felt it was part of God's plan that I'd be there for her to return the support she had given me when her son passed away.

Another colleague who I was able to come alongside to and give her support was an educational assistant who had suddenly lost her older adult son. I had worked and known her for years as I had been her younger son's history teacher, and both she and her husband had been supportive of me during my grief. I was glad that I could be there for her. Later, we formed a bond with each other, and we, at times, came together to help others on campus who lost their loved ones. We made ourselves available for the entirety of our remaining time we both worked at the school, and before our retirements, and we still communicate with each other on occasion.

Prior to joining our staff at school, another colleague who was our tech guy had lost his younger son. I had taught and coached his older son in baseball as well as coached his younger son who passed away in football. Before he began working at the school, he had been a professional sound man for performing bands, and I would contract him to set up the sound system for the graduation ceremonies that were my responsibility for a few years. When he and his wife lost their younger son, I immediately reached out to them. We created a bond not associated with work but shared while we are on campus, in that we were always aware of and appreciative of each other's shared loss. Having each other's presence on campus was helpful whenever either of us experienced a trigger and/or we needed to just be there for the other.

My presence on campus also allowed for me to be available for another fellow teacher whom I valued as a personal and dear friend. He was once on my staff when we both coached football, and he was a much loved and respected teacher on our campus as well as the community that our school was in. Before he retired, he had been a supportive friend when I lost my son, and sadly, I would be given the opportunity to return the favor.

My friend had just been recently retired and was no longer a member of our staff when tragedy struck both he and his wife when they lost their eldest daughter. Because of how much he meant to all of us still on staff, I took it upon myself the morning after she passed away to be the one to speak to all his closest former colleagues on the staff and give them the sad news personally. I just did not feel it would have been right to having the news announced or read during some hastily put together staff meeting or in-house email.

Now that he, too, is a reluctant grieving parent and we are both retired, we still meet occasionally with other former colleagues who have and continue to be there for the both of us. We do on occasion text or email supportive messages to each other, which ironically are usually perfectly timed to when either of us feels the need to hear a comforting word. I have also admired how he and his wife have carried themselves during their grief journey. They have set up a very prestigious memorial scholarship program in their daughter's honor, and they keep the memory of their daughter alive for not just themselves and their family but to all who knew her. And I admire how they have relied on their faith to walk through their grief journey together.

Because God saw fit that I remained at my school for the last ten years of my career, I was not only able to be of help for those whom I have just mentioned, but I was also made aware of others on my campus who may have had experienced losses—be it a child, spouse, siblings, parents, member of our student body, or any other close family members or friends. How can I not believe that it was God's plan that I would remain at my school for the remainder of my career? Perhaps God knew that I would be needed by others, so they could see that I was able to move forward with my grief. They could also see that in their grief, they were not alone, and that every day there would be a tomorrow. I can now see that there was a reason for me returning to work after my son died, it was because I needed to be a part of God's work in helping those who were in the beginnings of their own journey of grief, and in doing so, give thanks for those at work who also helped me.

> "For I know the plans I have for you," declares the Lord, "plans to prosper you and not to harm you, plans to give you hope and a future." (Jeremiah 29:11 NIV)

Chapter 20

Not Just My Grief

I have told you all this so that you may have peace in
me. Here on earth you will have many sorrows. But
take heart, because I have overcome the world.
—John 13:33 NLT

I would be remiss if I did not address my gratitude toward my former colleagues who provided additional support during the periods of time that my wife, Kirsti, had to endure her three bouts with cancer. These took place during the same period that I wrote about in the previous chapter. The challenges that I had faced when I returned to work and as I finished my career occurred concurrently as I also struggled with the emotional stress and concerns for my wife's health as she went through her cancer and its treatments.

There was never any question that I would be there to give my wife my full support, and yet, together still, Kirsti and I continued on without pause in our grief for our son Nick. Never once did we make it a second priority to the cancer, and with Kirsti's leading the way as an example, we always considered our grief for Nick to be our top priority. However, if it wasn't for the additional emotional and logistical support I received at my workplace, I am not sure that I would have had any inner strength left, following a long day at work to give to my wife what she needed from me, as she heroically and successfully did what she had to do in order to beat her cancer.

Some changes did occur at school with regards to how and by whom I was supported by through all that had befallen me with the addition of my wife's cancer. If anything, I found that, because more of my colleagues may have experienced cancer via a member of their family or perhaps themselves having gone through it, there was a loosening up of any reluctance on their part to approaching me as they may have done when it came to my grief. And don't let the "science" term in my professional position as a "social science" teacher fool you because I am not a man of great or, as far as I am concerned, any meaningfully competent scientific knowledge. As such, I felt cognitively lost at a time of my life when my brain had a hard time wrapping itself around the medical terms and the science behind the treatments.

At the same time, I felt helpless trying to understand enough of my wife's cancer diagnosis to be able to explain her situation to others coherently. The fact that there were others who I worked with who did have knowledge of and understanding about the workings of the human body and how it was affected by cancer and its treatments, it left me to appreciate their presence in my life at that time. I found them to be of great support and invaluable sources in helping me to understand just what it was that my wife was going through. And for that, I was so very thankful.

The emotions I had while working with my grief were real, and they surfaced in my everyday life often. But when it also came to my wife's cancer, I was so lucky to have had some of my closest friends available to me at work to talk with before school began, at lunch, and during breaks. At those times, those conversations would go back and forth between my grief and my wife's cancer, more often just them listening and giving me the avenue to breath while concerns over my grief and wife's cancer occupying so much of my waking thoughts. Nowhere were my friends support as important as when my duties at school, especially with athletic events, came into conflict with my needing to be with my wife for her doctor appointments, consultations, tests, and treatments.

At those times when I felt that I needed to be with her, I found that I could rely on my closest friends at school to help me to make it work. Those ladies and gentlemen all stepped up for me when I needed them the most, especially to cover my classes if I needed to leave school for a period or two during the day to be with my wife so that I could take her to her appointments or to retrieve her from a treatment or test so I could take her home.

In looking back, it was with my duties to the athletic department that I truly felt blessed for having them take time outside of the regular school day to be there for me. I was proud to have a cohesive and supportive coaching staff as well as my classroom teaching colleagues who, when I needed them, would be there for the beginning, middle, or conclusion of a contest in whatever capacity I needed them in. My administration also understood and supported me as I often had to attend out-of-town athletic meetings off campus, and they allowed me to have substitute teachers for my classes or covered for me in supervising contests until I could return to school to resume those duties. And of course, the office staff was always very supportive in helping me to keep the athletic program running smoothly if I was going to be off campus for a few hours while I tended to my wife and her needs.

In the previous chapter, I concluded that perhaps God wanted me to continue and finish my career at my school after my son's passing. I came to believe that, because there would be others who were grieving for their child or other loved ones, I was needed to be of support to them because of what I was going through myself. And together, through our shared experiences in working through our individual grief, we could feel assured that we were not going through any of our journeys alone. Therein is the love that God provided to me, and I came to realize that I was where I needed to be not just for others but that they too were meant to be there for me. And I am thankful for the blessing that was my workplace and my friends, whom I was grateful to work with while I was there.

> My command is this: Love each other as I
> have loved you. Greater love has no one that this:
> to lay down one's life for one's friends. You are
> my friends if you do what I command. I no lon-

ger call you servants, because a servant does not know his master's business. Instead, I have called you friends, for everything that I have learned from my father I have made known to you. (John 15:12–15 NIV)

Chapter 21

This Year's December

Whatever is good and perfect is a gift coming down to
us from God our Father, who created all the lights in the
heavens. He never changes or casts a shifting shadow.
—James 1:17 NLT

As grieving fathers, what should we make of the month of December? Is it the end of a year? One can argue that point as it is after all placed as the last month on the Julian calendar. As a former educator, I think I might be able to lay claim to December being marked as the half-way point of the school year. After all, my school years were divided by semesters, and as one semester would end, the second one would begin; and once the second semester came to an end, it marked the completion of the school year. But of course, that was usually end of May, beginning of June.

But for the secular world, December gives way to the sight of the festive decorations surrounding the Christmas and holiday seasons, giving a sense of a well-deserved end-of-year celebration to be topped off by an end-of-year party welcoming in the coming of another year ahead. But then as a Christian, December is the month that we celebrate the birth of Jesus Christ, reminding us of that singular event that we can trace the beginnings of our spiritual world and the never-ending journey that God has laid before us. But what about as a grieving father? Again, I ask, "What do we make of the month of December?"

In the world that we live in, all the above make for good definitions of what December can and may represent. For some, only one may apply, and to others, a combination, if not all, of them might apply. Before I truly came to Christ, I liked to think I was a combination type of guy. Depending on the mood, I thoroughly enjoyed the seasonal and commercial ambiance of the secular version of the holidays, but though I always recognized the importance of the original meaning of the birth of Christ, in the past I admittedly ended up more often attending the secular party rather than a midnight church service. But gradually, after I married and began raising children and even more so once I reluctantly joined the club of grieving parents, my definition of what to make of December began to evolve; and over time, it has redefined itself literally year by year.

What December has now become for me is a time to reflect on being thankful for getting through another year of grief for my son Nick. It provides me with time to see where I have experienced the highs and lows throughout my year and, to be honest, to see what forward progress in my grief journey I may have accomplished in the past year and what I may look forward to in the next one to come.

This year, being my thirteenth December since my son died, I do see that I have annually made positive progress in my grief journey. Don't get me wrong; any positive forward movement in my grief never takes away from the occasional triggers that still remind me of what is my loss. But as the years have moved forward, I am able to embrace the memories of happier times of when Nick was with us than the unhappy moments during the time that I lost him. More importantly is how to this day, he still plays such a major role in my life, my happiness, and my hopes for a future that I know will eventually include our reunion in heaven in the presence of God.

During those early years of my grief, the month of December was such a hard journey to get to, and once it arrived, it was also a very hard month to get through. But as the years have progressed to the present, Decembers have become easier to get through, and I am finding them more comforting as I recall the ones I had with Nick.

Where at first the memories of Christmas past only brought me tears and pain for the joy I felt would no longer be a part of my life, the tears have now gradually been joined by the smiles brought on by the triggered memories of happy times.

I now find that my Decembers remind me of just how much my son loved the holidays and how the joy he found in them were so infectious to us all and, in many ways, have become infectious to us again. For Nick, the holiday season began with Halloween, progressed through Thanksgiving, lit up his world during Christmas, and concluded with the celebration of his mother's birthday shortly after the new year. But as you may have already guessed, the happiest and most joyful period during the entire holiday season for Nick was always Christmas.

Nick loved everything about Christmas. He loved the colors of the Christmas decorations, the music, and the holiday foods and sweets, especially if chocolate was involved; and I think what he enjoyed the most was both the giving and receiving of presents. I see now more than ever that God provided me a gift in allowing me thirteen years of experiencing just how much Nick could truly find joy in either a spiritual or secular Christmas. From Nick, I can see the true meaning gained by the beauty and wonder of Christmas celebrations—be it in church listening to a choir singing "Silent Night" or in walking through the mall and hearing the catchy Christmas jingles such as "Santa Claus is Coming to Town" over the loudspeakers.

And as for the topic of Christmas jingles, Nick and I shared a love of what has been one of my favorite secular Christmas songs for years—"Little Saint Nick" by the Beach Boys. I like to think Nick loved this song because his transplanted Southern California dad did, but more likely than not, he was just as enamored by it because his name was in the lyrics. And after a couple of years of trying to avoid hearing it, it is now once again a go-to song for me to get myself into the mood of the holiday seasons as I play it over and over in my car or on my computer. And I can once again listen to it anytime—be it during the day, before bed, or even on my cell phone when I am out walking the dogs.

Prior to Nick's passing, when I heard the playing of "Little Saint Nick," I knew that Christmas had arrived. Now, over time, it has returned to a prominent place in my heart, and I can't help but feel that Nick's infectious joy over Christmas still lingers inside of me. I now find myself enjoying what was once Nick's version of Christmas joy once again, and seeing the part that God has played in it has kept Nick alive in my heart and returned me to happy times once again.

The first years after Nick died saw the secular Christmas that I enjoyed as a child, and later as the father of two wide-eyed sons, almost disappear. And I know that any father in my place, at whatever level they are in their grief, may find it hard to bring back the Christmas they once knew when their entire family was whole and present. But as the years have progressed, my heart has begun to reopen and look forward to December rolling around again. I am learning once more to enjoy my new normal and to accept how it shapes my last month of the year.

A new normal does not mean that many of the traditions of the past can no longer still exist; it only means that you now look at or approach them differently. And as for a family Christmas, a new normal may include old traditions revived, new ones created that help you to move forward, and allowing for some old ones to be kept in some type of emotional storage—perhaps to reintroduce at another time or perhaps to stay locked away for good.

Now I can look at my years of grieving during Christmas and see that as time has progressed, my wife and I have been able to renew some of the traditions we had previously built together as a married couple and as parents. We have returned to some of those traditions that had once brought our family joy and now do so once again. But truth be told, we have admittedly not returned to all of them, some out of respect to our late son Nick or because to avoid some of those triggers that we have learned we no longer need to revisit or they do us no good to emotionally relive them. And though we knowingly have limited from the past some old traditions that may still cause us pain, we also have taken into consideration what Nick loved to do, and that helps to bring cheer to our eyes in honor of him.

The return of December as a happy month has many factors by which I am indebted to for its return to my heart. First, there was the return to our hometown of my older son, JP, who had moved out of state to pursue educational and career goals. JP returned to his hometown after having married his wife, Kimberly, and he brought our grandson, Nicholai, with him as well. Their presence has been a major factor in allowing me and my wife to renew many of the Christmas traditions that JP, Kirsti, and I had shared with Nick.

The house once again is on display with decorations, letting our world know that the Contreras's Christmas spirit is back! I have returned to staying up late on Christmas Eve to watch the movie *It's a Wonderful Life* as was my personal tradition before January of 2011, when Nick went to heaven. My Mickey Mouse waffles have also made a comeback as our traditional Christmas morning breakfast, and our grandson has stepped in admirably and with the same wide-eyed joyfulness his uncle Nick once displayed by taking place as the family Christmas morning Santa Claus. In that role, like his uncle Nick did before, he is in charge of handing out the presents that sit under the tree, continuing the traditional duty of the youngest member of our family.

By bringing back of some of our family traditions, I have come to believe that Nick, in some way, has given us his blessing to resume Christmas as before. I also believe that he has influenced me over the past few years to begin new traditions that have taken on a personal note within me and have led me to a closer relationship with my son in spirit, one that I feel I was never able to attain with him when he was here on earth with me before.

One such new tradition I now celebrate each year falls on every Christmas morning in the predawn darkness. What has now become my own annual pilgrimage finds me waking early before the dawn on Christmas day to drive to my church, where I sit on a cold and sometimes wet granite bench dedicated to Nick in the church sanctuary. There I will sit, talk to him, cry a bit, and together as father and son—me on the granite bench and he from heaven—we will watch the Christmas morning sunrise, often joined by a lone bird that appears almost immediately following the first light of day. As the lone bird sits on a branch above me in one of the trees, I feel a symbolic presence that I believe is a gift from God with a Merry Christmas message from my son.

I can now look back on my soon-to-be past year of grieving for my son Nick, and I can see that more and more tears are giving way to more and more smiles. I can now see a lot of the sadness eventually giving way to more happiness, and I see that the absence of my son now gives me more purpose to keep him alive for those of us who knew him. I can see that this past year of living and growing in my grief progress has led me to look forward to each new December in my annual journey. And I know that God has used my year to pave a path for me to continue to live for my family, my friends, my fellow grieving fathers, and my son Nick.

This is the day that the Lord has made; let
us be glad in it. (Psalm 118:24 ESV)

Chapter 22

•••◦•——————•——————•◦•••

December to December, December

Give thanks to the Lord, for he is good. His love endures forever.
—Psalm 136:1 NIV

As I look back over my shoulder at the year I have recently left behind, I realize that the lifelong year-to-year grieving for my son Nick will always be a part of my life. Each December as I reach the end of another passing year, I once again reflect on how my grief journey for my son has progressed. Every year, I see positive forward movement; and I see that, with time, I have become emotionally stronger, more compassionate, more honest, more empathetic, and more loving. With the luxury of time, I can see more clearly the path that God has set forth for me to follow in order that I may better serve him while still grieving for my son. I can see that the best path I can choose is the one that leads me to live for those that I love through God, and in return, he allows me to keep my son Nick alive for the remainder of the time he has planned for me while I am here on earth.

My intention in writing this book was to share how as a grieving father I have walked through my year at various paces of speed, sometimes with my head held high and my eyes wide open and at other times with my head down and my eyes closed shut. Sometimes on good days, I can see that the path is clear and smooth ahead, and on the not so good days, I am slowed by unexpected obstacles that have made the journey rougher than anticipated. But whenever the road seems tough, I have made up my mind to trust that God will navigate me and my progress through the complicated mazes and help me to reach the destination he has always pointed me toward safely. As I have spent a good part of this past year writing this book, I can easily compare it to walking on a forward journey and moving toward the end of a planned path. And as my path has a final destination, so does this book have a final chapter. My final destination for this year was to guide this grieving father, meaning me, to reach this final chapter and to move toward my year's final objective so that I could celebrate the end of one journey and to begin looking forward to a new one.

In the first chapter of this book, I opened up with the story of taking my grandson on a cold and damp December evening to one of his swim practices. In sharing that story, I compared the experience to the many times I did the same with his dad; my older son, JP; and his uncle, my younger son, Nick. But as I observed the actions and behaviors of my grandson in the pool, it had a triggering effect on me.

At that moment, I couldn't help but close my eyes, allowing the voices and efforts of my grandson and his teammates in the pool to bring back memories of watching my son Nick working out in that very same pool, under pretty much the same conditions. With sincere fond memories in my thoughts, I imagined once again seeing him doing something he enjoyed and did well, recalling with pride what I felt for him then and how I feel for my grandson now.

The trigger that I experienced that evening was unlike many of the others I had received before. The trigger I had that night was not a sad one, but if anything, it brought a smile to my lips and a happy memory to my heart. After taking my grandson to McDonald's after his practice, as I had promised him I would, and then dropping him off at his house, I returned home and sat at my computer before going to bed, taking time to reflect on that evenings emotional trigger at the pool for my son. With Christmas a few days away and the new year soon to follow, I found myself looking back on the year I was about to exit, and I realized that getting through to the end of the year was becoming less and less difficult than it had been in the earlier years since losing my son.

After the holidays were over, I began writing this book with every intention of having the first chapter be called "January." However, once I started writing, I soon realized that the story I wanted to share at the beginning of the book was the recollection of how my grandson's swim practice triggered pleasant memories of my son Nick's similar experience.

As told in the first chapter, the story had taken place last December at the end of what would soon be the conclusion of the year we were about to exit. By opening the first chapter about my grandson's swim practice and the trigger that followed, it helped me shape how the rest of the story would influence not just the new year we were about to enter but also the days, weeks, and months that would follow.

Once I began to write what I thought would be the final chapter of this book, I knew it was the right decision to share my December story in the chapter before the "January" chapter. After all, who says that a year in my life can't be from December to December? But as I finally got to writing the final chapter, I changed course and chose instead to highlight how much my son loved the Christmas season and how his infectious demeaner toward the month of December had begun to spread on me once again as it had when he was here. What I had found was that, in the most recent years leading up to this December, I have begun to welcome whole heartedly the return of many of the old traditions prior to Nick going to heaven. And in every instance, I could feel my son's presence in each Christmas tradition that my family has revived.

So the book that I meant to be about a year in the life of a grieving father, from January to December, became the same story from but from December to December. Eventually, it has evolved into what it is now, which is the same story but from December to December, December. And in each December, you see that my son

Nick's presence in all three chapters has shaped the beginning, the middle, and the end of my year.

So it was decided that the tone of this book was to be set during the first chapter, and it would end with not one but with two December chapters. As I have gone through my year in each chapter, I can reflect how each month reminds me of previous years past. And where I used to dwell with remorse on how my relationship with my son, which to my distress had not been what I had hoped it would be prior to his going to heaven, I now see that the tears have become less and are now being replaced more often by the smiles of happy memories past. Though it may sound strange, I have found that God has provided for a special relationship between Nick and me to grow and that it will last forever.

Much is written about waves that can trigger your emotions when it comes to grief, and I have learned through GriefShare to encourage others how, when waves of emotions come, to try to roll with them. By encouraging them to roll with the waves, my prayer is that they will learn as have I, that at some point the waves will not be so rough, and they will be able to navigate them again. The late Jimmy Buffet said as much when he compared grief to waves—or, as he called it, the wakes behind a boat. This was his description of grief:

> Grief is like the wake behind a boat. It starts
> out as a huge wave that follows close behind you
> and is big enough to swamp and drown you if
> you suddenly stop moving forward. But if you do
> keep moving, the big wake will eventually dissi-
> pate. And after a long time, the waters of your life
> get calm again, and that is when the memories of
> those who have left begin to shine as bright and
> as enduring as the stars above. (Jimmy Buffet)

The thing about grieving as a father is that grief will be a constant in your life; it will come and go every year. It doesn't go away, and it only moves on to the next year. But each year has its months, and by living from week to week each month and day to day each week, you will learn to roll with the emotional waves that come with that constant reminder that your child is not there with you anymore. But take heart with time. As the memories keep rolling in like the waves, you will find that as each month gets you to the end of the year, they will get easier to navigate.

Those triggers that were once painful and that I, at first, tried hard to avoid but often failed to do so, I have found at some point that they became more bearable. And for a grieving father like me, I now have come to welcome some of those triggers because they have brought to me the reminder that the memory of my son's presence here on earth is so much more powerful and meaningful than the sorrowful moment when I lost his physical presence to heaven. Many of those triggers now allow for me to never forget that I am still proud of him and that I still love him. Note the present tense.

I wrote this book to share how a man like myself, the father of a son who now resides in heaven, grieves for him throughout every single year of my life. I wanted to share how over the years I have learned to work through the struggles of emotional pain and sadness, only to give way to returned happiness, joy, and love—not just for those who are still with me here on earth but also for my son Nick who resides with the Lord. I wanted to show other grieving dads who are in my same position how thankful I am for God's presence in my life and how he has been there for me yesterday and today, and he will be there for me tomorrow. But more importantly, I wanted to share how God has made it clear that I will always have my son's continued presence in my life.

I now believe that the presence of my son has never truly gone away, and though he may be in heaven now, I am confident in the knowledge that I will join him there later. Having said that, I also believe that God has given me many paths to choose from during my grief journey, and with each path of my choice taken, I can see the forward movement in my grief progress. With each year, my journey has allowed me to retain my sanity, my earthly hopes, and my continued love for those whose prayers are for me to make it through each leg of my journey. And like anyone who completes a journey and looks back at the path recently taken, I choose to look back to where I have been, how I have successfully made it to the ending point of this past year, and in the process, how I have set myself up for my continued journey into the next new year to come.

What I have confirmed after each year's grief journey is that my son Nick lived a full and complete life. I know that he was loved by so many and that he is still loved by the likes of me, his mother, his brother, and many of our family and friends. And I see that he has influence on some of my life's decisions and on my approaches to loving and helping others and especially the members of my family and fellow grieving parents.

From last December to this December, as I made my way through another year of grief for my son, I have felt my relationship with him grow. Where I once mourned for and regretted the relationship that I had hoped to have with him and that I was sure I had lost forever, I was happy to be wrong. Over the years, as I have missed having him and his physical presence here on earth, I have come to realize that the most important relationship that I have with my son is the same one God has always provided us from the first day I lay eyes on him, and for the thirteen years, I got to watch him grow. And I now know that God's intention was that Nick and I would be in a father-son relationship forever. The relationship that God has gifted me allows me to close my eyes whenever I want, and with love in my heart, I can proudly say to Nick, "I am still your dad, and you are always my son."

Love bears all things, hopes all things,
endures all things. (1 Corinthians 13:7 ESV)

About the Author

 David Contreras is a retired high school teacher, athletic director, coach, and the author of the book *Forever 13* through Christian Faith Publishing. Married for thirty-seven years to his beautiful wife, Kirsti, he is the father of two sons and the grandfather to one grandson. Thirteen years ago, tragedy struck both Dave and his wife when they lost their thirteen-year-old son Nick, changing their lives forever. Since then, with the support of family, friends, and those who have walked alongside them during their grief journey and through their faith, they have committed themselves to keeping their son alive in their hearts, as well as others who knew and loved him. In doing so, they find purpose in walking alongside other grieving parents who have or are experiencing a similar fate.

It is through his writing, public speaking, and his participation as a volunteer facilitator with both GriefShare and a monthly fathers' bereavement group that David feels led to providing support to other parents who may feel they are alone as they too progress through their own grief journeys. Making no claims to being an expert at grief survival, his hopes are that by sharing his own experiences, others will find that they, too, can get through this unnatural experience of losing a child. And they don't have to do it alone because God will provide.

9 798889 428699